The Answer Machine

Synthesis Lectures on Information Concepts, Retrieval, and Services

Editor
Gary Marchionini, *University of North Carolina at Chapel Hill*

Synthesis Lectures on Information Concepts, Retrieval, and Services is edited by Gary Marchionini of the University of North Carolina. The series will publish 50- to 100-page publications on topics pertaining to information science and applications of technology to information discovery, production, distribution, and management. The scope will largely follow the purview of premier information and computer science conferences, such as ASIST, ACM SIGIR, ACM/IEEE JCDL, and ACM CIKM. Potential topics include, but are not limited to: data models, indexing theory and algorithms, classification, information architecture, information economics, privacy and identity, scholarly communication, bibliometrics and webometrics, personal information management, human information behavior, digital libraries, archives and preservation, cultural informatics, information retrieval evaluation, data fusion, relevance feedback, recommendation systems, question answering, natural language processing for retrieval, text summarization, multimedia retrieval, multilingual retrieval, and exploratory search.

The Answer Machine
Susan E. Feldman
2012

Theoretical Foundations for Digital Libraries: The 5S (Societies, Scenarios, Spaces, Structures, Streams) Approach
Edward A. Fox, Marcos André Gonçalves, and Rao Shen
2012

The Future of Personal Information Management, Part I: Our Information, Always and Forever
William Jones
2012

Reading and Writing the Electronic Book
Catherine C. Marshall
2009

Hypermedia Genes: An Evolutionary Perspective on Concepts, Models, and Architectures
Nuno M. Guimarães and Luís M. Carrico
2009

Understanding User-Web Interactions via Web Analytics
Bernard J. (Jim) Jansen
2009

XML Retrieval
Mounia Lalmas
2009

Faceted Search
Daniel Tunkelang
2009

Introduction to Webometrics: Quantitative Web Research for the Social Sciences
Michael Thelwall
2009

Exploratory Search: Beyond the Query-Response Paradigm
Ryen W. White and Resa A. Roth
2009

New Concepts in Digital Reference
R. David Lankes
2009

Automated Metadata in Multimedia Information Systems: Creation, Refinement, Use in Surrogates, and Evaluation
Michael G. Christel
2009

The Answer Machine

Susan E. Feldman

ISBN: 978-3-031-01152-8 paperback
ISBN: 978-3-031-02280-7 ebook

DOI 10.1007/978-3-031-02280-7

A Publication in the Springer series
SYNTHESIS LECTURES ON INFORMATION CONCEPTS, RETRIEVAL, AND SERVICES

Lecture #23
Series Editor: Gary Marchionini, *University of North Carolina at Chapel Hill*
Series ISSN
Synthesis Lectures on Information Concepts, Retrieval, and Services
Print 1947-945X Electronic 1947-9468

The Answer Machine

Susan E. Feldman

SYNTHESIS LECTURES ON INFORMATION CONCEPTS, RETRIEVAL, AND SERVICES #23

ABSTRACT

The Answer Machine is a practical, non-technical guide to the technologies behind information seeking and analysis. It introduces search and content analytics to software buyers, knowledge managers, and searchers who want to understand and design effective online environments. The book describes how search evolved from an expert-only to an end user tool. It provides an overview of search engines, categorization and clustering, natural language processing, content analytics, and visualization technologies. Detailed profiles for Web search, eCommerce search, eDiscovery, and enterprise search contrast the types of users, uses, tasks, technologies, and interaction designs for each. These variables shape each application, although the underlying technologies are the same. Types of information tasks and the trade-offs between precision and recall, time, volume and precision, and privacy vs. personalization are discussed within this context. The book examines trends toward convenient, context-aware computing, big data and analytics technologies, conversational systems, and answer machines. The Answer Machine explores IBM Watson's DeepQA technology and describes how it is used to answer health care and Jeopardy questions. The book concludes by discussing the implications of these advances: how they will change the way we run our businesses, practice medicine, govern, or conduct our lives in the digital age.

KEYWORDS

search engines, content analytics, user interaction, natural language processing, contextual awareness, probabilistic computing, big data, analytics, conversational systems, enterprise search, Web search, eDiscovery, eCommerce search, unified information access, InfoApps, machine learning, adaptive systems, answer machines, IBM Watson

"The sky won't fall, and what if it does?"

For my parents, who taught me to live, think, question, and write.
For David and Elana, who taught me everything else and who keep me laughing.
For Bob, who holds up the sky.

My love and gratitude

Contents

Preface

In 2011, a very clever machine from IBM named Watson defeated two human champions in the quiz game, Jeopardy. Watson is an answer machine, and its Jeopardy win was proof that it could be done. The press was immediately abuzz: would machines replace humans? Would we need teachers, programmers, or writers in the future? Could we automate doctors?

The short answer to these questions is no, we still need people. But the better question to ask is how to join man and machine so that we can address more complex problems than either can manage alone. Machines excel at performing repetitive tasks. They don't get tired and they don't get bored. They are good at crunching vast amounts of information to find patterns, whether they make sense or not. They have no emotional investment in theories, and are consistent to a fault. They don't get embarrassed if they return the wrong answer. Machines, however, are very bad at making the intuitive leaps of understanding that are necessary for breakthrough thinking and innovation. Humans excel at this kind of thinking. People can balance the imponderables that are almost impossible to program: diplomacy, subtlety, irony, humor, politics, or priorities. People are good at making sense of data and synthesizing ideas. Above all, people can understand and make exceptions to rules. Machines can't. We need people to make decisions, but we need machines to help us filter through more information in order to make better-informed decisions. People need this assistance because they are swimming in an overwhelming sea of information, and need time to think if they are to innovate and act wisely.

For this kind of help, new types of more "intelligent," language-capable machines, like IBM's Watson, are a necessity. Marrying intelligent machines with humans holds great promise: machines to do the repetitive work and forage through massive amounts of information looking for patterns and evidence to support or reject hypotheses, while humans supply the necessary judgment, intuition, and system override to determine which patterns make sense. This collaboration divides up the work into what each party—machine or human—does well. Anything that follows a predictable pattern is a good candidate for automation. Health care tasks are a good example of this duality: let the machine enter diagnostic codes based on existing rules. Let advanced information systems find the latest research on treating illnesses. Gathering information, organizing it, weighing the probability of its pertinence to a particular patient—this what a Watson does well. This frees clinicians to work with patients, assess the evidence and use it to improve patient care.

Watson is an answer machine. Part search engine, part artificial intelligence, part natural language technology, and stuffed with the specialized information to answer questions on a specific subject, be it medicine, finance, or Jeopardy. Answer machines sift through mountains of information to find patterns. Although they don't make complex decisions that try to balance costs, emotional aspects, or ethics, they free up humans to do what machines can't do: consider the factual and the non-factual and then make well-informed choices. They provide better answers, faster, than current search engines do. Watson is one visible, well-publicized example of an answer machine, but there are many others that are arriving on the scene, albeit with less fanfare. Search engine technologies – the focus of this book – have undergone a metamorphosis of their own. The simple search engine of the 90's, which matched keywords and phrases, has been transformed into a multifaceted access point to all kinds of information—in multiple formats and from a multitude of sources. Indeed, today the term "search engine" is a misnomer. Like Watson, search today comprises more technologies than keyword search: categorization, clustering, natural language processing, database technologies, analytical tools, machine learning, and more.

This book examines the metamorphosis of search from its awkward command line youth to the emergence of something much more complex, something I call an answer machine. The following chapters look at the role that information plays in the work and personal lives of people today, the tools we have developed to interact with digital information, and the future for these technologies as they move from engineering marvels to everyday tools.

INTENDED AUDIENCE

The Answer Machine is a practical overview of search and content analytics technologies, their uses today and their role in the future of computing. It also explores user-information system interactions: how and why people search for information and the online tools that they need in order to do so. It is not intended for programmers and developers. Rather, its purpose is to introduce buyers and users of these technologies to the concepts of search and text analytics technologies and their uses, and to offer some practical guidelines of selecting appropriate software. The last section discusses the future of information access, the promise of answer machines like IBM's Watson, and the impact of trends like the shift to probabilistic computing, big data, business analytics and unified information access. It concludes by speculating on how these trends will change how we do business, practice medicine, and interact with information in the future.

Susan E. Feldman
August 2012

Acknowledgments

My heartfelt thanks to the many people who were instrumental in shaping my career, and who were my cheerleaders in the writing of this book. First to my editors, Stephanie Ardito and Elana Feldman, who mopped up stray commas, run-on sentences, and lapses in logic. Also to Bob Feldman, mentor in all things mathematical, and willing factotum.

My gratitude to Hadley Reynolds and Jon Lehto, who reviewed and consulted on multiple drafts of The Answer Machine. They generously slogged through the manuscript, found holes, suggested fixes, and contributed ideas.

I would not have been able to write this book without the help of my mentors, Elizabeth Liddy, Barbara Quint, Stephanie Ardito, and Win Sewell. Each of them listened, taught, and encouraged me at various turning points in my career. My thanks to all of you.

Members of the search industry have been unstinting in their willingness to discuss and explain search and content analytics technologies. They helped me to glimpse the future, and then think practically about it. In particular, I am indebted to members of IBM's Watson Division for reviewing and commenting on the section on IBM Watson and Answer Machines in general.

I thank my colleagues at IDC, particularly Tony Picardi, Steve McClure, and John Gantz, who encouraged me to tackle big ideas.

Finally, my thanks to Gary Marchionini and Diane Cerra, who enticed me to write a book and then were patient until it materialized.

Susan E. Feldman
August 2012

CHAPTER 1

Introduction

Information. We collect, organize, barter, buy, sell, and talk about it. Information is the social currency we exchange in our personal and work interactions. It's how we get to know each other, how we advertise ourselves to the world. Information is engrossing and entertaining, not just informative. Although there may be more of it now than in the past, the online world hasn't changed our need for information, although it has certainly increased the number of information channels with which we interact.

Information consists of the signals from our environment that we use to understand our world. Humans absorb information from their surroundings constantly. Although this book focuses on information in its electronic form, the term "information" can't be limited to only documents and data. Information is a gesture, a raised eyebrow, a quizzical look, or the smell of a newborn child. We spend a lot of time and energy collecting and organizing our information. Whether that organization is formal or not, we categorize information implicitly in order to manage our lives efficiently. We separate items into what we need to pay attention to, and what we can ignore. We learn the salient characteristics of trees, food, people, poisons, vehicles, etc., so that we can apply rules for how to deal with each. In a formal sense, we create systems for organizing, preserving, and finding our information so that we don't have to remember it all, and so that we can share it with others: books, libraries, documents, databases, search engines, and soon, answer machines. The implicit categories are dynamic: they shift and evolve as our experiences and interests change. And the categories are personal, built from our particular interests and experiences. The challenge is to build formal systems that are also dynamic and that mirror how we think about the world, but on a general enough level so that they are usable by more than one person. If we can understand how we need and want to interact with information, then we can design better systems that support this inherently human activity—creating, exchanging, collecting, and analyzing the information that's important to each of us in order to understand our world.

1.1 WHY INFORMATION SEEKING IS SO IMPORTANT TO US

People have always tried to make sense of their world. We look for patterns—"are there more red M&M's in a bag than there are brown? How come there are no purple ones?" And we construct reasons for why this is true "Maybe people don't like brown M&M's…maybe purple dye is expensive…"

Because information seeking and sense making is so much a part of being human, most of us have become quite sophisticated in our techniques. Our fascination with information and our need to exchange information with each other carries over to the digital world, and in that environment, our needs have not yet been met. We can look for direct answers to questions, but finding the "why" is much harder. "Why" requires exploration, discussion, and interaction. We need to amass information, then look for patterns and relationships in the data. We might want to create or test theories and then find evidence to support or reject them. In order to find "why" we must be freed from the strictures of the search box to let patterns and relationships like cause and effect bubble up from the data. Much like a doctor looking for the reason for a patient's elusive pain, we must poke, prod, and consider before we can arrive at the best guess for the cause.

Today, we have amassed a wealth of information, but our interaction with it is impoverished. We have yet to move our human model for easy information foraging and exchange, exploration, and discussion to the online world.

CHAPTER 2

The Query Process and Barriers to Finding Information Online

2.1 THE QUERY PROCESS

Let's begin by looking at the information gathering cycle. No matter how or where we look for information, the process is the same: we identify something we need to know; we figure out how and where to ask for it; we formulate an initial question. Once we have our beginning question, we pose it to a potential information source, be it human or electronic, to refine and clarify the question. Finally, we receive an answer. If that answer solves our problem, we go on about our business. If it doesn't, we try again.

This process works well in the human-to-human world. For instance, suppose I am driving down the street in Boston on a lovely summer day. I'm lost (I'm often lost in Boston). I see someone walking down the street. I lean out the window and say, "Can you tell me where Summer is?" The person immediately understands because of the context of the question that this is not a philosophical inquiry. She says, "Do you mean Summer Street, Summer Place, or Summer Lane?" "Oh," I say, "Summer Lane." "It's at the second light on the right," she replies. I continue on my way.

Notice that this interchange, while common, has several important elements:

1. It's a conversation. It is continuous. Each comment builds on what went before.

2. Both parties understand the context implicitly: I am driving and look puzzled; it is summer.

3. The question is ambiguous because "Summer" has several meanings.

4. The person who answers the inquiry removes the ambiguity of season vs. name of street because of the context in which it is asked.

5. The conversation is an "information negotiation:" the two parties negotiate the meaning of the question before an answer is returned.

In contrast, finding information online is very awkward:

1. It is not continuous, using the previous interaction to refine the current one.

2. There is little or no shared context, making it impossible for an online system to implicitly understand the reason for the question.

3. The ambiguity of the question, "Where is Summer?" ensures that the online system will return answers for all the meanings of the query term, "Summer."

4. No information negotiation can take place because the system is not interactive. It can't engage in a dialogue to narrow down the question, although today, it might offer a list of possible phrases that include the word "summer." The implicit clues that humans use to understand a situation—the season, the person in a car looking lost—are information that would have to be explicitly described to an online system.

When we are dealing with words, nothing is ever straightforward. Words have multiple meanings and there are many ways to express the same idea using different words. For these reasons, the search process hits a bump almost immediately: what does the searcher mean? What is she really looking for? To compound the problem, searchers are often searching for information on a topic that they know little about, but documents are written by authors who are steeped in the terminology of the field. So, searchers ask for "high blood pressure," while authors write about "hypertension." Without a full understanding of what the searcher wants, a search engine can only return a set of matches to a query, making a guess at the underlying information need. Simple matching of

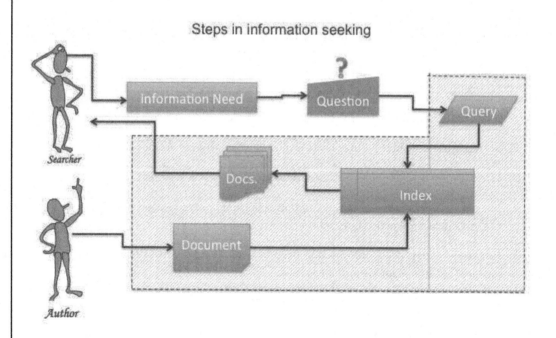

Figure 2.1: Steps in information seeking.

query to documents makes it difficult to return the best or most expert answers. For this reason alone, today's search engines are not answer machines. They are query matchers. And people are notoriously deficient in asking for what they really want—with good reason—because they often don't really know what they are looking for until they see it.

In a typical online information system, shown in Figure 2.1, a searcher formulates a query that may or may not reflect his underlying information need. The imperfect query is sent to a search engine, which matches the query with whatever documents in the index contain the same terms. Today's online information seeking process looks like this, with both the searcher and the author excluded from the matching process, with little opportunity to negotiate the search terms in a human-like dialog.

The process appears straightforward. Our searcher asks a question. It's sent to a search engine that returns the documents or facts that best match the query. But as we have seen in the human-to-human example, people use multiple clues to help each other arrive at a mutually agreed upon question before they ever go looking for the information. Finding the right question turns out to be the crucial first step in getting the right answer.

2.2 QUERY PROBLEMS

Words are both the grist and the major stumbling block for search. Writers delight in nuance and variety. Computers are very literal minded. Ambiguity is rife unless the system can—like people—understand not only the context of a word within the surrounding text, but also the knowledge of the real world that people carry with them. Keyword matching search engines take each word at face value—a string of letters to be matched, no matter how that word is used. But most words have more than one meaning, and conversely, there are a myriad of ways to express each idea. More advanced search engines try to interpret which meaning of a word is intended by looking at the context in which a word is used, but unlike documents, queries provide little or no context for what the searcher is seeking. The following are examples of the barriers search engines run into in attempting to return good matches to a query:

- **Probe queries**. Probe queries are initial, very general queries that sound a search system to see if it contains any information at all about a topic. Searchers may start with a broad query to find out what the possibilities might be, even though they have something specific in mind. The empty search box gives them no hints on how to enter an effective query. These probe queries are a valid approach to triangulating on information in the human world, but they often go awry online. For instance, a searcher looking for a picture of an African frog of a specific genus and species might begin with a probe query for "biology." This is so broad that the searcher is overwhelmed with 179,000,000 results. At that point, he needs help in refining the query and also exploring the collection to figure out how to find what he really wants. In a human-to-human information interaction, we would first negotiate what it was that he was looking for. Online, however, the probe query is not a precursor to refining a search. It is the search. Even asking for frogs may be too broad. One will still get treatises, poems, and odes to frogs rather than the color image that was the goal of the search. Worse, the right document might never have the word "biology" in it. It is more likely to discuss "amphibians."

- **Lack of user context**: It's impossible to tell from a short query *why* a searcher is asking a question. In fact, the same query from the same user can require different answers during the course of a task. E.g., if I am planning a vacation, I may want pictures of Indonesia, some history, and major sights when I enter "Java" initially. Today's search engines may help me disambiguate that search by asking if I mean "coffee" or the java programming language, but they can't tell what kind of information I want without understanding where I am in my information gathering process. Several weeks later, having decided where I want to go in Java, I will want flights and hotel information, not a list of places to visit, but I will still type in "Java."

- **Short queries.** One-word queries, and even two-word queries don't give search engines enough information to remove the ambiguity of a term. The query needs to be disambiguated (which meaning of the term is the right one?) and expanded (by adding synonyms) in order to return better results. (See the section on word ambiguity below.)

- **Misspellings.** Spelling trips up some very smart people. Typing trips up everyone. When I typed "biology" in the example above, it came out "bilology." How's a poor search engine to know? Today's search engines are able to suggest some spelling corrections, but they can't untangle them all.

- **Alternate spellings, alternate terms.** British and American English use different spellings for some relatively common terms: aluminium/aluminum, theater/theatre, gray/grey. British and American usage can also differ wildly for common terms like: elevator/lift, truck/lorry. A search engine that matches only on what is typed in would return incomplete results if it simply matched the query it received.

- **Acronyms.** Another source of common misunderstanding, acronyms may refer to multiple entities or objects, depending on which industry or subject domain they come from. SVM is a support vector machine in information retrieval, but it's also the ticker symbol for Silvercorp Metals, Inc.

- **Punctuation and diacritics.** Common usage varies in how writers approach some common abbreviations. VP and V.P. are both used for vice president. Accent marks in French or diacritics in the Slavic languages may need to be eliminated (normalized) when they are indexed. Both "Dvorak" or "Dvořák" must be retrievable no matter how a query is entered or a document is indexed. Language recognition and Unicode encoding are necessary if a search engine is to index non-English text. Even in English text, documents can include non-English.

- **Proper nouns and case sensitivity.** Few search engines distinguish between proper nouns and those in lower case, for good reason. We find capitalized words in European languages at the beginning of every sentence, but they aren't necessarily proper nouns. Conversely, people who are searching for a proper noun often don't capitalize it in their query. Search engines therefore rarely distinguish upper case and lower case usage, unless they also use content analytics to extract names of people, places, and things. In the European languages, proper nouns—names—are capitalized. This helps us distinguish the concept, "autonomy," from the company, "Autonomy" (now part of Hewlett Packard). However, in the sentence, "Autonomy was important to him," we have no way of figuring out whether this is Autonomy the company or autonomy the concept. For that matter, without the context of the surrounding text or discussion, people can't figure this out either. One of the worst problems in the technology field is "IT" (meaning information technology), which is parsed as "it," a stop word (a word that is customarily not indexed because it is so common).

- Word ambiguity:

  - **Too many meanings**. Most words have more than one meaning. Consider how many ways you can use the word "table" or "fly," or "bank" or "charge," or "seat," for instance. This phenomenon of multiple meanings is called "polysemy." For example, the word "pool" might be a verb—"pool our money." It might be part of a noun phrase—"swimming pool," "gene pool," or "betting pool." The process of figuring out which of these meanings is the right one is called *disambiguation*, and it requires some give and take between the searcher and the system if there is no text other than the query, "pool." Search engines today may offer a list of possible phrases in order to get the searcher to disambiguate a query by expanding it to a phrase. The search engine may also attempt to disambiguate a term by looking at its context. The words that co-occur help to define each of the constituent terms.

  - **Too many synonyms**. We delight in saying the same thing in as many different ways as possible. English, in particular, gives writers a wide choice of expressions for any idea. Good writing practice mandates that we not repeat the same term over and over again, but find another way to express an idea. The better the writer, the more the variety. This creates headaches for searchers who must try to guess how an author phrased a concept. We need retrieval systems that match ideas, not words. In addition, different regions of the world or different subject specialties may use different terms to mean the same thing, such as *lorry* and *truck*, or *elevator* and *lift*, or *pump* and *impeller*, or *hypertension* and *high blood pressure*. In an exact match system, we miss important works if we don't ask for these other synonyms.

  - **Terminology mismatch**: Experts and laymen may describe an idea or concept quite differently. A "heart condition" may be referred to by doctors as "congestive heart failure," or, worse, by the acronym "CHF."

  - **Anaphora or co-reference**. One of the devices we use in writing is to use a pronoun like "he," "she," or "it" to refer back to a person, place, or thing that we mentioned in a previous sentence. Search engines and especially sentiment monitoring systems need fairly complex instructions in order to tie the specific noun or proper noun to the pronoun in a succeeding sentence. This becomes important if we are trying to figure out what someone's opinion is about a topic: "I was initially skeptical about using a bike helmet. Then it saved my life when I was knocked off my bike." In this case, we need to tie the "it" in the second sentence to the "bike helmet" in the first.

– **Phrases**. Phrases in English tend to remove ambiguity, as we demonstrated in the example of "pool," above. However, determining whether a group of words constitutes a phrase or what its boundaries are is difficult for a search engine. For example, "*John, a tree surgeon and my brother-in-law's sister's son, was responsible for cleaning up the results of the storm with his chain saw.*" In this sentence, you have phrases within phrases, some of which modify John, and some of which modify the storm. The word "saw" without the modifier "chain" could easily be classed as a verb.

– **Irony and sarcasm**. Search engines are notoriously poor at detecting irony and sarcasm, just as literal-minded people are. Queries are rarely sarcastic, but documents often are, and the sarcasm of a simple statement like, "*You can insist that he's a good senator until the cows come home, but it won't change my mind,*" could easily be mistaken by a search engine for a statement about cows.

– **Metaphors**. Metaphors make language colorful, and well-written text is often rich with metaphors that create headaches for search engines. For example, war images are often used to describe sports and politics. Terms like "*battle,*" "*win,*" "*campaign,*" or "*fight*" are liberally sprinkled throughout documents on these topics. A query like "*Senators win*" looking for news about the Ottawa Senators hockey team might return both articles about the hockey team and the US Senate, as shown in the following Google search (Figure 2.2):

Senators win fourth in a row - Fox Sports   msn.foxsports.com/.../Ottawa-**Senators**-top-New-York-Islanders-040... Apr 1, 2012 – Kyle Turris scored twice and had a pair of assists, Milan Michalek added his team -leading 35th goal and the Ottawa **Senators** clinched a ...
GOP **senators win** concessions, but state budget still faces ...   www.kbia.org/.../mo-gop-**senators-win**-concessions-state-budget-still-... 2 days ago – Nine conservative Republican **senators** who held up debate on Missouri's budget plan had claimed it spent too much, relied too heavily on ...

Figure 2.2: Google search: "Senators win."

The next section of this book discusses the evolution of technologies that have been developed for information seeking—search and content analytics—and how they handle some of these problems.

CHAPTER 3

Online Search: An Evolution

Information access and management technologies have evolved separately for the worlds of structured and unstructured information, but they all have the same goal: to gather, organize, and store information so that it is findable and usable in the future. This is true of database and business intelligence (BI) applications in the structured data world and of content management, search and content analytics technologies in the world of unstructured information. However, the very nature of structured information vs. that of unstructured information mandates different techniques for managing and retrieving each type of information. Numbers are precise in their meaning, so precision and consistency are the goals for storing and retrieving information in database applications. Search and content analytics, however, must handle the unpredictability of text and other media like images or sounds that can't be divided neatly into rows and columns. Languages and images are nuanced and rich because there are so many ways to express the same thing. But this variety of expression makes it difficult for a machine to recognize similar ideas or pictures across synonyms or sunsets.

Designing software that can accommodate the human urge for originality and variety is not easy. Search and content analytics technologies must interpret words, sentences, documents, and chat postings that range from elegant metaphors to curt semi-literate ramblings. Therefore, these technologies must allow a certain latitude, or fuzziness. While linguistic variety is laudable, retrieving everything about a topic, while eliminating everything that is extraneous, requires language understanding in order to find synonyms, ignore metaphors and irony, and understand cause and effect in a sentence. Search engines must do more than return matching strings of letters if they are to find precisely what a searcher is seeking in the fuzzy world of language. While this poses a complex problem for designers of search and content analytics software, it is not as daunting as it seems at first. Language has structure, even if it isn't the rows and columns of a database. Babies who are just learning a language are able to do so because they perceive patterns and relationships among words.

3.1 HISTORY

Search and content analytics technologies have a long history, although their use has become widespread only in the last decade. Early search engines matched the words in a query to words in documents, very much as SQL commands in databases do today. The "grep" command in UNIX or basic SQL commands are good examples of the assumption that if you ask for something, you know what you are looking for, that you can spell it correctly and phrase it so that a search engine can understand what to retrieve. Search developers quickly found that retrieving words was very different from retrieving numbers. Individual words occur unpredictably. Search engines must accommodate words that occur in sentences, sentence fragments, and even in images. Even if language has predictable structure and patterns, and we can predict word frequency within a collection of text, we are a long way from pinning down who will use exactly what word when. With this degree of uncertainty, was there some way to make language computable and searchable?

In the 1960's, two approaches to information retrieval developed in parallel: traditional online systems and statistical full text search engines. The first group—early online publishers of professional journal literature like Predicasts, National Library of Medicine, or ABI/INFORM—were modeled on the database approach to information, and used a schema or standard template for each record in their databases. Each document was described with the same set of fields (e.g., title, author, subject, source journal, and date) and the descriptions were formatted consistently using thesauri and name authority lists. The records were created manually by professional indexers. When search technology improved to handle larger volumes of text, searchable abstracts were added to some of these databases, although full text searching was not yet possible.

NASA's STAR, Dialog, LexisNexis, Orbit, and others aggregated these online collections to provide a single point of access to multiple sources. Even if the indexing varied from one database to the next, professional searchers learned the correct terminology for each, and merged results from multiple sources manually. Access was expensive and required training in the Boolean commands to search. Because of the high online fees and the exacting nature of the training, librarians and other information professionals acted as intermediaries for end users.

These collections of professionally reviewed, indexed, and abstracted documents were relatively small: the bibliographic record plus a short abstract that was written by an expert. They were therefore very consistent in their use of indexing terms and in the format of the author/title/source fields within each database or source. Searchers of these online systems were professionals: highly trained and talented in crafting queries that would get high quality, precise results. In order to use these sources, end users needed to work with an information professional—an intermediary—to explain what they were looking for. As professional searchers became more and more adept, and their online sources started to add full text, the command languages became more complex and varied so that searchers could stem a word like aluminum to "*alumin*" in order to return "*aluminium*" as well as aluminum. Searchers were accustomed to grouping sets of synonyms in order to retrieve documents that might describe a concept in various ways. For example, to locate an article on "*what was left out of Windows 95*" in *PC Computing Magazine*, a Dialog search might have looked like this:

s jn=pc/comput? and microsoft/ti and (left()out or omit?) and
windows/ti and py=1995

Searchers kept lists of the states or countries or cities within a geographic area in order to retrieve France, Belgium, UK, Denmark, Norway, Sweden, Italy, etc., in a quest for information on manufacturing in Europe.

In summary, these early online systems offered high quality, but less abundant materials that were carefully curated. They depended on the expertise of the publishers, the abstracting and indexing services, and the professional searchers in order to retrieve what end users were looking for. And they were expensive, often with an hourly access fee plus a per-record fee that forced searchers to use unnatural strategies like overly precise queries that returned short format citations in order to curb expenditures.

The second approach to information retrieval came from computer science, particularly the work of Gerard Salton at Cornell University. In the early 1960's, computers lacked sufficient horse-power to crunch through large amounts of text. Documents needed to be represented in some sort of mathematical surrogate so that they could be compared efficiently to a query and to other documents without bogging down the system. System designers also realized that exactly matching a query to a document was not sufficient for good text retrieval because of the multiple variations that authors use for describing a topic. Vector space models were developed by Salton for the SMART Information Retrieval System, and are still prevalent in information retrieval today, particularly in Web search systems. These algebraic models represent documents and queries as vectors in an imaginary multi-dimensional information space. One might imagine this representation as a set of lines extending at different angles from a central axis. Each angle is a different topic. Queries on the same topic should have roughly the same angle as a pertinent document, so they can be matched correctly.

Vectors consist of all the significant terms (as well as any other metadata) in a document or query, and form a vector, or line that extends into this space in a direction that represents a topic. This mathematical approach assumes that the words in a document can be used to determine what the document is about, and that the more closely a document vector matches a query vector, the more likely they are to be about the same topic. Because the words don't have to match precisely in order to create similar vectors, it's possible to retrieve documents that are similar to a query without exactly matching it. This is known as fuzzy matching. It's also possible to find clusters of similar documents in a collection by grouping documents according to the distance of the angle between their vectors. A number of document collection browsing systems are based on vector space models.

Unlike the exact match Boolean systems, these "fuzzy match" systems returned both exact matches and those that were partial matches, thus retrieving materials that might be of interest to the searcher even though they didn't fulfill all of the parameters of the query. However, because of the larger sets of results, it became important to present the results with "best matches" first. Thus, relevance ranking was born. Although it may seem counterintuitive, tests we ran in 1998 [Feldman, 1998] demonstrated that fuzzy matching often out-performed exact matching even in searches for known items. Memories are faulty and even known item queries can omit information—like the proper field name that is necessary for an exact match. Statistical and probabilistic systems returned more documents, and sometimes found documents that were highly desirable that were missed by exact match systems.

Finding similar documents, as well as exact matches, was a breakthrough in information retrieval. But when collections of documents became too large, it was equally important to return sets of documents that were organized with the best matches to a query first so that the searcher did not have to wade through too many results of uncertain value. In the 1970's, Karen Sparck Jones developed a method for measuring the relative relevance of a document to a query. This measurement, called TF/IDF or term frequency over inverse document frequency, first counts the number of times a query term appears in a document (term frequency). Then it compares the document to the collection as a whole (IDF), with rare terms receiving a higher weight than common terms. This second measure helps to distinguish one document from another. Terms that are rare in the collection receive a higher weight, and boost the relevance of a document. In other words, if a term appears frequently in a document, but infrequently in the collection as a whole, then the document is considered to be highly relevant to that topic. For example, in a collection of cancer research documents, the term "tumor" would receive a low weight because it occurs in so many documents. However, "GIST" (gastrointestinal stromal tumor), is a relatively rare term, so that searches for GIST would rank documents with that term more highly than if it were equally weighted with "tumor." This concept is still used widely for relevance ranking in Web search engines and others, although it has been modified to include knowledge about the frequencies of terms in a language, and other factors that improve the notion of relevance.

As computers added capacity, other approaches to finding relevant matches to a query became feasible. Probabilistic systems use pattern matching, categorization, and machine learning to calculate the probability that a document will match a query based on the patterns of words within a document. The system is trained with documents that are good examples of a topic. Then at query time, the system looks for the best matches to that pattern. For instance, when the word "car" appears with terms like "railroad," "train," "track," or "caboose," it is probably about a railroad, while if it appears with "seatbelt," "road," "mileage," or "tire pressure," it's probably about an automobile. Probabilistic computing and its implications will be discussed in more depth in Chapter 6.

Since those early information retrieval systems, fuzzy matching has become an indispensable part of the larger information access system for both unstructured and structured information. Along the way, most search engines, particularly those geared for enterprise use, have added new technologies and tools such as categorization, clustering, natural language processing, and even database and business intelligence features.

3.2   THE SHIFTING INFORMATION LANDSCAPE: 2000-2012

The human drive to seek information, coupled with the pervasiveness of personal computers and growing access to the Internet, created a perfect environment for the explosion of the World Wide Web and Web search engines. The Web unleashed a torrent of information, and invited anyone with a computer and an Internet connection to become a searcher.

3.2.1   END USERS AS SEARCHERS

End users search differently than intermediaries do. Unlike intermediaries, end users know what their ultimate information needs are, and they recognize the right answer when they see it. However, they may have difficulty crafting a suitable query. End users are also less likely to create long, well-formed queries In contrast, intermediaries are proficient at query formulation, and in helping end users pinpoint what they are seeking. But an intermediary can only craft a query based on what he is told (or suspects). End users are less hung up on precision, and more willing to browse (but less willing to plow through pages of results). There are some logical reasons for this: the end user knows what's in the back of her head, even if she can't phrase it effectively. End users are rarely trained in search syntax for professional online systems, and are also prevented from using these systems because of the high costs. They are rarely skilled searchers. More importantly, the end user has an entirely different motivation for searching from that of the information intermediary. Intermediaries pride themselves on searching effectively. Crafting a good query is important. Satisfaction comes from retrieving the information and presenting it to the end user. That's the end of their task. End users, however, are searching for information in the course of completing a much longer process. They need to find what they are looking for in order to get on with the real purpose of the job: find a statistic to complete a document, find a hotel to plan a vacation, find a review in order to purchase a camera. Systems that are designed to satisfy the intermediary's need for a well-formed query won't satisfy the exploratory, often vague and messy needs of the end user.

To accommodate end users, online systems needed to move from expecting a finely crafted query to supporting information exploration. It became obvious to online system designers that they had to incorporate what they knew about good human search practices into a new kind of retrieval software to index and retrieve this vast, quickly changing volume of information to accommodate the unpredictable searching skills of millions of new users. Neither careful curation of the collection nor professional intermediaries could handle the expectations of end users for quick access to current information. Technologies that could bake professional searching expertise into the search system were required. In short, although search engines could analyze text and create an index of terms to search against, they also needed to do what professional searchers had been doing instinctively:

- Stem words so that we could retrieve alternate spellings, plural and singular forms

- Expand queries with alternative terms, add synonyms and variant spellings

- Disambiguate terms with multiple meanings by using noun phrases or adding context

- Unite names like IBM and International Business Machines and Big Blue to return better coverage of a company, place, or thing

- Expand place names like Europe or Northeast US to include names of cities, countries, provinces, and states within a geographic area

- Understand the difference between proper nouns and the same word as a common noun (Delta the airline company vs. delta of a river)

- Find the same concept no matter how it is expressed

- Do all of the above intelligently and unobtrusively by making suggestions, or by showing other potentially relevant results in addition to perfect matches.

3.2.2 CHANGES IN INFORMATION SEEKING

In the past decade, with the advent of the Web and free access to a world of information, the worlds of personal and workplace information seeking have drawn together. We have seen a metamorphosis in the way consumers and workers find and use information. People expect to do their own searching either at home or in the workplace. The lines between work and home have blurred as people tote around tablets and smart phones so that they are constantly in touch with their families, their friends, and their work, no matter where they are or what else they are doing. Not only are they constantly communicating with each other, but they are seeking information: "Siri, find directions to the nearest coffee shop." "Are any of my friends there?" This means that information seeking now happens in all kinds of contexts, and on all types of access devices and formats.

Between 1995, when the Web was just emerging, and 2005, we saw a shift from information professionals to end users as the primary users of online information systems. Now, nearly twenty years later, valuable information is often freely available on the Web, and end user searching has won. End users may not be adept searchers, but they do know what they are looking for, and can recognize it in a set of search results, even if they haven't formulated their queries very well. They like the control of being able to browse, and the serendipity that doing your own search brings. Many academic authors have finally been freed to publish directly, and publishers have knuckled under to the end user movement and started to post at least subsets of their holdings. This is a mixed blessing. It takes the typical end user a fair amount of time to find information—IDC's surveys show that most knowledge workers spend 6-10 hours a week searching for information, and are only successful roughly a third of the time [Feldman, 2009]. This extra time to find information, like so much else, has been bundled into the lengthening work week for most professionals, so that it is rarely counted as an expense by most enterprises. A consequence of this trend is that many company libraries have downsized or closed, and information professionals have moved to other positions or retired. Web search engines have by far outpaced other information sources. Social sites, something that didn't exist in 2000, have begun to compete with Web search engines as information sources. And what about those high quality, professional, fee-based online services? Only 17% of the end users surveyed reported that they used them in 2010, in contrast to the 26% who reported using them in 2002 [Feldman, 2010].

Lost in the shuffle, temporarily, are two key services that professional intermediaries provided: helping end users define what they are looking for, and understanding the provenance of the located information so that trustworthy information is provided to the end user. Both of these functions are difficult to automate effectively, but newer information applications are certainly taking a stab at both.

Although they are now comfortable with online searching, end users are not necessarily satisfied with the results returned either by Web search or enterprise search. When Google changes its ranking algorithm, the ranks rebel. Businesses suddenly lose customers when they are no longer in the top 10 results. Users are unhappy if they don't get the results they expect. Here's a message from Rachel Happe in 2011 about a change in Google's ranking algorithm that gave top priority to her posts on GooglePlus, a social forum. This change in ranking is a good example of a search engine's design choice that results in unintended consequences:

> "When I Google myself, the things I share on G+ come up first in search results. This is a very weird search experience because I'm pretty sure if people are searching my name, they want a general overview of who I am and/or my contact info... seeing a picture of my daughter or some other random content I shared on G+ leaves a very weird initial impression. This makes me uncomfortable because the only people who are really going to search on my name are people who don't know me very well, generally speaking. It's like entering a cocktail party and saying "I hate email" (which was my latest G+ update until this morning)... very odd human behavior that is now being codified with technology."

> —communication from Rachel Happe

Happily, Google listened to the outcry from annoyed Google Plus users and changed the algorithm to just show the user's profile, not the random postings.

The consequences of the shift from professional information seeking to everyone as a searcher have been mixed. Certainly, access to a wealth of information has changed how we live, enabling us to accomplish simple tasks like finding directions, making dinner reservations, or looking up stray facts no matter where we are. Furthermore, end users will recognize the information they are looking for, even if they haven't crafted a perfect query, while intermediaries don't have that underlying information need firmly fixed in their heads—they are interpreters. On the other hand, distinguishing between "good" and questionable information is not easy, so scams abound, and decisions are made on incomplete, old, or wrong information, creating information disasters (Horton). It's hard for most people to judge what's authoritative and what's not. Everyone is now a searcher, but our research shows that their success rate is fairly low. The result is that people are swimming in information, rumors are rampant and hard to squash, and business decisions are often made on skimpy evidence.

Today we are on the cusp of yet another revolution in information access, this one moving us to pervasive information that is integrated within the flow of whatever else we are doing. We can decide to see a movie, find reviews, view a trailer, buy tickets, and get directions—all while everyone involved is walking to a coffee shop, sitting around the breakfast table, or on the phone. Pervasive information moves us away from information as a separate destination and back to what is more natural—exchanging information when we need it to complete a task.

3.2.3   STATE OF THE ART TODAY

We now have forty years of experience in designing online information systems. Search technology is no longer experimental. Analytics for text is well developed. Many of the challenges are clear:

- Searchers have difficulty formulating the right question

- Voluminous collections of information are hard to navigate and analyze

- Language is ambiguous and hard to interpret for literal-minded computers

- Interfaces are still experimental—their effectiveness varies with the user, the user's task or context, and the user's background and expectations

- Images and speech are hard to retrieve because they are even more subjective, variable, and difficult to represent than text

- Speech (voice) and gestures are natural carriers of information, and need to be incorporated into interaction design

These challenges shape the direction for search technology research today and for the next decade. There is no question but that information access systems have evolved to support end users in their quest for information, and that they have moved away from expecting a trained intermediary to perform complex searches. Today's search and discovery tools, for both Web search and enterprise search, are aimed at people who frame queries inadequately, but who will recognize what they want when they see it. Search is only one starting place among many in the quest for information. The emphasis now is on designs that allow users to browse, explore, and discover within a specific work environment that is based on a process or task.

These newer search-based applications, which we call InfoApps because they address information-centered processes, may also include collaboration tools, publishing tools, marketing tools, sales tools, business intelligence tools, and predictive modeling. InfoApps, are designed around a specific process like eDiscovery, marketing, or Web publishing. They create comfortable information work environments that integrate multiple technologies so that workers have at hand all the tools they need. This is in stark contrast to traditional work environments today that require knowledge of multiple tools and information sources in the course of completing a task. InfoApps have tuned the search and analytics technologies for a particular process: find an answer, find the best answer, find all possible answers, or even, "what's here and what should I know about that I don't already?" InfoApps have taken off because they make people's lives simpler, aggregating technologies and related information in one easy-to-use environment.

CHAPTER 4

Search and Discovery Technologies: An Overview

4.1 ONLINE INFORMATION ACCESS SYSTEMS

Unlike books on a shelf, digital information is malleable. It is almost infinitely sortable. It can be divided, mined, distributed, published, republished, and archived in dozens of places (or more) simultaneously. The technologies to store and manage information run the gamut from databases of fielded records to search engines to even more complex systems that provide access to both structured and unstructured information.

Databases and data warehouses impose the same order, or schema, on all the records before they are accessed, making it possible to find all instances of widgets sold in October by price, part number and region. They return matches to an exact match query quickly, as long as the query matches the schema.

Search engines and unified access platforms identify and extract meaningful elements—words, phrases, metadata—in documents and other data sources, and then create an index of all of those extracted elements. The list of terms in the index is not organized into categories or schemas. At query time, the index finds and returns any documents that contain some or all of the terms that match the query. The more advanced systems also return matches to the concepts or ideas, based on word patterns and synonyms. This kind of information retrieval excels in returning matches when the query is ad hoc—not matching a predetermined schema. Both approaches have their place.

The structured approach is typical of database and data warehouse technologies: predictable structures in which each record contains the same type of information in the same format; the columns of the database or schema give the context needed to understand what any specific number might mean. Unstructured information, or content, is not amenable to this approach because the content and format of a document, including the sentences and paragraphs, are unpredictable. Databases provide context to each record by supplying a standard schema so that, in an inventory database, for instance, all the numbers in column 1 are product names, in column 2 part numbers, in column 3 prices, and in column 4 are number of each part in inventory. Even though the figures or amounts may be the same in two different columns, the schema provides the context to interpret whether they are dollars or number of items in stock. In contrast, text, images, and music provide context and meaning through their surrounding words, pixels, or notes. Remove a word from a document, and you don't know whether "car" means a railroad car or an automobile. For this reason, search and content analytics technologies have had to develop a different approach to finding and analyzing unstructured information so that the context surrounding a word is not lost.

4.2   SEARCH AND DISCOVERY TECHNOLOGIES

Search technologies and content analytics have several elements in common:

- They are language-based and meaning-based: they attempt to understand the meaning of a query, a document, a phrase, a sentence, or a paragraph so that the user is connected to the information he seeks. The basic element that is processed by a search engine or content analytics application is understandable to a human.

- They are designed for human interaction. Because they are language-based, they enable human-machine dialog. The potential of using dialog for helping users define a query, ask a question with normal speech, and explore an information space with a more comfortable interaction design is only now being explored. Apple's Siri is the first widespread experiment in conversational systems, but it will change the expectations of the marketplace that is now inured to poor information interactions.

- Probabilistic or statistical matching, sometimes called fuzzy matching, rather than exact matching, distinguishes these technologies. Fuzzy matching returns all matches to a query, whether exact or approximate. For example, for the query, "*presidential candidates in 2012*," I should get documents containing "presidential candidates," but also those containing "candidates," "presidential debates," "candidate for president," and in the more advanced systems, even some that contain "Obama" or "Romney," and none of the original query terms because these names co-occur with "presidential candidates," and have been identified as being pertinent. As we've noted, there is no one right way to phrase an idea. Language technologies must handle this variety by returning the exact matches but also the good-but-not-perfect-matches to a query. The effectiveness of fuzzy vs. exact matching has been amply demonstrated in the TREC Legal Track (Text Retrieval Conference, sponsored by NIST), which tested exact vs. fuzzy matching systems in eDiscovery. Fuzzy matching finds relevant documents that exact match systems miss.

- They must disambiguate terms by using each term's "context," a fuzzy concept in itself. How much context is necessary to distinguish one meaning of a word from another? A sentence? A paragraph? Or must we also add in external knowledge about the user's interests and activities?

- These systems are based on computational linguistics, a science built on the assumption that linguistic patterns are predictable and computable.

- Knowledge bases that include basic rules for syntax, dictionaries for meaning, word lists, specialized taxonomies, and ontologies improve these systems' accuracy.

- These systems assume that they will return large sets of potentially relevant information that will need to be explored and sorted through. Mechanisms like relevance ranking, clustering, categorization, faceted search, and visualizations are a requirement.

- Search and discovery technologies provide ad hoc information access. They do not require schemas or pre-structured reports. Instead, they extract the elements of meaning from documents and other sources and combine them at query time.

All of these aspects of the search and discovery technologies are familiar, but their import goes far beyond the boundaries of search. Today, with vast amounts of information—both structured and unstructured—to be processed, analyzed, and understood, the need to discover the unexpected, to uncover patterns, and to predict outcomes relies on a probabilistic approach that retrieves information that is close, but not perfect. As we move from the "deterministic" approach that is familiar to the world of databases and predetermined schemas to probabilistic computing with its emphasis on discovery, scenarios, and levels of uncertainty, what we have learned in developing search and content analytics technologies is very applicable.

"Search" consists of an assortment of tools and technologies that create access to collections of primarily unstructured electronic information. We can divide these technologies roughly into two groups. The first—search engines—return a set of documents that match a query. Basic search matches a query against each document in a collection. Once matching documents have been found, most search engines display the documents in relevance ranked order, with the most relevant document displayed first. Relevance is calculated using a combination of the TF/IDF measure, discussed in the previous chapter, with other factors such as the "popularity" of each document, which is based on the number of "clicks" the document has received for similar queries. Patterns of co-occurring terms that indicate what a document is about may also be used to predict its relevance.

The second group—content analytics—extract the elements of meaning from each document: names of people, places and things, time, location, sentiment and opinion, and the relationships among these extracted elements: facts and events, cause and effect, definitions. Content analytics is used to tag documents to improve search accuracy and create browsing interfaces. Because these technologies extract facts, they are useful in question answering systems like online self help or customer support sites. They deliver the pertinent bits of information that may answer a question like "how do I fix my leaky printer cartridge?" Content analytics are also used to explore collections of information and to find relationships like drug side effects, ties between crime syndicates and terrorists, the influence of a blog posting on the political process, or the opinions of travelers about hotels. Content analytics are the basis for building exploratory tools like browsing interfaces, visualizations of relationships, or timelines of events.

In summary, search engines are document-oriented. They return lists of documents that match queries like, "Get me a list of hotels in Boston." Content analytics, in contrast, look across documents to find smaller information particles than documents—words, phrases, names of people, places, and things, time, opinions, or ideas. Content analytics extract information elements and their relationships to each other to enable exploration and analysis across documents, sometimes without an overt query: "What are our customers complaining about?" "Where are the innovative ideas in our organization coming from?" Both provide pathways through a collection of information, but they serve different purposes. In both search and content analytics, however, results are tied back to the originating document so that the context of the extracted information can be verified.

4.3   TYPES OF SEARCH SYSTEMS

Within the context of this book, I will refer to information retrieval systems that use Boolean matching as **traditional systems**. Traditional DIALOG or LEXIS-NEXIS are examples. Boolean systems are based on Boolean logic. They use operators such as AND, OR, NOT in mathematical statements. Boolean systems are exact match systems. You get what you ask for. If you ask for *rebellion* and *Rwanda* within ten words of each other, and a document contains *rebellion* and *Rwanda* within 11 words of each other, you won't retrieve it.

 Statistical or probabilistic systems predict the relevance of a document to a query using statistical algorithms based on the frequency of occurrence of terms and sometimes the word patterns that are typical of a topic. Probabilistic or statistical systems identify exact matches to a query, but they also use probability and statistics to return good approximate matches as well. In these systems, you get what you ask for, but you might also get what you *should* have asked for. Unfortunately you will also retrieve documents that contain the query terms but not the information you wanted. These systems will return documents that contain *rebellion* and *Rwanda* as long as either appears in the document, although they will display those that contain both terms before those that contain only one term.

 NLP or Natural Language Processing systems use knowledge of language structure and meaning in order to match queries to documents. NLP systems, depending on the depth to which they use linguistic tools, should be able to parse a full sentence query such as, "*When did the rebellion in Rwanda start and who are the leaders of each faction?*" In a query such as this one, the NLP system would know that you are looking for a date ("*When*"), the identity of the people involved ("*Who*"), of a rebellion in a specific location (i.e., Rwanda). NLP has already captured the blocks of meaning, like names of people and places, and it should be able to translate "when" into a request for a date. NLP systems excel in queries that give them real text to chew on. Today, pure NLP systems are used most often within specific domains to answer questions in finance ("tell me about this company"), customer relations, or online self-help. Because the semantics, or meaning of the words, are the basis for these systems, adding specialized terminology like names of products, people, or companies improves their ability to return excellent matches. Confining them to a specific domain also removes ambiguity: you are unlikely to want more than one meaning of "bank" in a financial system.

 In reality, it is possible to combine all of these approaches. Most systems use some linguistic technology for identifying the language of a document, finding word boundaries, and stemming words automatically. A Boolean system could easily return relevance ranked documents. Many statistical systems use some NLP features to identify proper nouns. They may even look like they understand meaning when they offer related words in a "concept search." What they are really doing is giving you a list of other words that occur frequently within the same documents that contain your query terms.

4.4 THE INFORMATION RETRIEVAL PROCESS

In very broad terms, here's how an information retrieval system works. We will examine the technologies used in this process in more detail in the next section.

Step 1. Ingestion. At this stage, documents are analyzed to identify language and word boundaries. They may also be categorized and tagged with metadata to indicate title, source, and various linguistic structures (see below, sections on the search index, categorization, and NLP).

Step 2. Indexing. A basic text retrieval system consists of three separate files: the file of full records or full text documents, including all bibliographic and indexing information; the dictionary, which is an alphabetical list of all the unique words in the database, and an inversion list, which stores all of the locations of occurrences for each word in the dictionary. This structure is called an **inverted file**. Searching very large databases is efficient with this file structure, since each word in the dictionary is an entry point for beginning a search. The structure of the inverted file is essentially one big table, which avoids the joins that slow down relational databases. To control file size, the index doesn't contain the full text of the documents in the index; instead, it consists of *pointers* to those documents, which are stored elsewhere.

New documents are interfiled into the existing list, so that the system has all occurrences of every word in one place, with their positions within each document. Increasingly, text retrieval systems also add or create knowledge bases with internal lexicons, semantic networks, or lists of phrases, synonyms, and personal pronouns. The index, which is used for matching, need not be on the same server as the full text file. This architecture reduces server storage requirements.

Step 3. Query parsing. When a query arrives, it must be interpreted appropriately for the system. In Boolean systems, this is not as complex an operation as it is in full NLP systems, since the searcher has already phrased the question in computer-interpretable terms. NLP and statistically based systems must do some of the work that searchers originally did in preparing a query. A statistical system may modify and expand query terms by automatically looking for word stems, singular and plural forms. It may also assign weights to each term. A full NLP system tags all the parts of speech and identifies objects, subjects, modifiers, phrases, and verbs. It also may expand geographic terms as well as add synonyms and alternate forms for proper nouns. Then it creates an unambiguous representation of the query for the system to match against its knowledge base. A partial NLP system might identify stems, synonyms, and proper nouns and then create a query representation.

Step 4. Query matching. The interpreted query is matched against the inverted file and the knowledge base, if there is one. Traditional online services match each query word exactly as it is entered, in the combination specified by the searcher. Thus, if we ask for *global()warming*, we will get *global warming*, but not *warming around the globe*. Statistical systems will get us global warming as a single phrase, but also any document that contains *global* AND *warming*, as well as *global* OR *warming*. A full NLP system might be able to match the query: "What evidence is there for global warming?" with documents on climate change that do not contain the phrase, *global warming*.

Step 5. Search results prepared and returned. Once all the candidate documents are selected which match the query, they are sorted by date, by field, or by how relevant the document is predicted to be to the query. Traditional systems commonly return results sorted in reverse chronological order, but they could sort in ascending chronological order, by author's name, by report number, etc. Statistical and NLP-based systems typically return documents ranked in descending order of relevance to a query. Where these systems vary is in how they define a "close match." How to present search results is one of the hottest areas of information retrieval research today. Lists of documents, relevance ranked or not, are still prevalent. However, new directions in how to design the search engine results page (SERP) include presenting the information in a table, aggregating information, and presenting it as an answer, or presenting the list of documents with the beginnings of a dialog "did you mean ___?" as a rudimentary conversational system.

Relevance ranking is determined by first assigning a weight to each term. This weight is determined by how frequently the term appears in the document, and also by how often it occurs in the database as a whole. Relatively rare terms in the database that occur frequently in a document are assigned a higher weight than words that are more common. Documents that have more occurrences of the query terms, and in which the terms appear closely together in the text are ranked highly. Usually (but not always) a document that contains all the query terms will be ranked higher than one that contains fewer terms but more appearances of those terms. Variations in how factors are weighted account for some of the differences in how search engines perform. Some of these factors might be the position in the document where the terms occur (title, chapter heading, bold print), how closely the terms appear together in the document (proximity), or whether the emphasis is on matching all the terms or on number of occurrences of one of the query terms. There is no reason why any system can't return documents sorted by any criterion. A Boolean system could add relevance ranking, and a statistical system could return documents in order by date.

4.5   SEARCH AND CONTENT ANALYTICS

We can group the technologies associated with "search" into four broad categories:

- Connectors and crawlers

- Search engines

- Categorizers and clustering engines

- Content analytics and natural language processing

Together, these technologies gather information, index it, and provide access to it. Each of these technologies provides different pathways into a collection of information. Taken together, and tuned for a particular application, they provide a user experience—and answers—that is far superior to the common user experience today. The trick is to select the most appropriate technology for each use. Chapter 5 discusses these technologies in terms of the types of uses, sources, and users.

4.6   COLLECTING INFORMATION FOR SEARCHING OR ANALYSIS

Crawlers collect documents from sources such as the Web or enterprise repositories by following URL's or addresses. In other words, they crawl along the filaments of the Web that lead from one document to another, collecting the contents of each document along the way. For obvious reasons, this process is also called spidering.

Connectors collect information from collections of information that do not have addresses, like databases or content management systems. The name is something of a misnomer in that they are more than simple information conduits. They transform queries into the appropriate query syntax for each information source. Depending on the information available in each source, the connector submits a search form, if required, manages authentication, retrieves search results and parses them. Smart connectors may map similar search fields or concepts to each other between sources, performing a sort of database-like "ETL (extract, transform and load) for content," even if the terminology differs from one source to another. For instance, smart connectors should be able to map "customer" in one database to "client" in another, normalizing and tagging information so that search engines can perform concept searches across all sources.

4.7   SEARCH ENGINES: THE INDEX AND THE MATCHING ENGINE

Search engines match queries to documents. Because of the ambiguity of language, while search can certainly find exact matches, as databases do, it is usually better to return partial matches as well so that alternate expressions of the same idea will be presented. This process is called "fuzzy matching." It enables search engines to return matches for misspellings, alternate spellings, two out of three query terms, documents in the same category, etc. Fuzzy matching helps to correct for the ambiguity of language, but it also injects a note of serendipity into a search so that searchers can find related materials that they may not have thought to ask for. It also means that searchers don't have to specify the parameters of their query precisely. Fuzzy matching turns out to be invaluable for solving a number of information problems today, like de-duplicating standard relational databases, or detecting patterns of fraud in the financial services industry.

Search engines have two major parts—the index and the matching engine. They may also be highly integrated with categorizers, content analytics, crawlers, and connectors. However, these latter can be purchased separately, so for clarity's sake, we will consider them to be separate products.

Indexing engines create a large index to all of the documents in a collection. Like a back of the book index, the index can be thought of as a table that consists of all of the words in all of the documents in a collection, with the location of each word in each document. The documents themselves are pointed to from the index; they are not part of it. Because this index, sometimes referred to as an "inverted index," is a single table, searching through it is very fast, making it ideal for searching large collections of information that change quickly. Unlike relational database tables, the inverted index doesn't require a schema or joins across tables. Usually, words that are so common that they can't differentiate one document from another—like "the," "is," or "from"—are dropped from the index. These are called "stop words" because they are stopped from being indexed. Removing stop words from the index reduces the size of the index and speeds up retrieval. However, stop words are important structural elements in language (see section on syntax below). As we will see, dropping common verbs, articles, and prepositions from the index limits the scope of what we can retrieve using an inverted index. A search engine that eliminates them can't find "To be or not to be."

The philosophy behind creating a large indiscriminate index of everything that will be combined at query time is an important one because it complements the database world of carefully crafted schemas. Databases organize information before it is queried. Search technologies essentially use the query as a basis for organizing information on the fly—a sort of "instant data warehouse" that is tailor made to answer the information need. Search indexes are all-inclusive because they can't predict what question they will have to answer. Although they don't require a schema that is designed to answer predictable questions, they certainly can and do make use of such schemas if they are available. Where search indexes shine, though, is in assembling information from disparate sources on demand, making it possible to answer unexpected questions immediately, without having to create a new report in order to deliver the information. Today's indexes can also be updated incrementally as new information arrives. That's also an important point—search indexing and querying does not have to be a batch process, depending on the need for up-to-the minute information.

Search or matching engines match queries to terms in the index. They parse an incoming query, using the same technology that was used to create the index. Let's assume that the query is "*boston history*." A basic statistical matching engine would look for all occurrences in the index of the word "*boston*" that are next to or near any version of the word "*history*" (e.g., "history," "historic," "historical").

4.8 PRESENTING THE RESULTS: WHAT IS "RELEVANCE?"

Information seeking has two broad goals: to find all the information that is relevant to a query, and to leave out any information that is not relevant to that query. As is the case with most sweeping statements, the devil is in the details, for defining relevance is not a straightforward problem. Relevance tends to be in the eye of the beholder; it is rooted in the information need of the moment. Take the query, "Boston." Do I need a simple map showing where Boston is? Which Boston are we talking about, anyway? There are six "Bostons" in the US alone. And if I want information on Boston, Massachusetts, am I interested in hotels, restaurants, flights to Boston (from where?), Boston history, concert schedules, or the Boston Red Sox? The easiest thing to do—and what a human would do—is to ask the searcher to define what they need. That's what tomorrow's answer machine will do. Unfortunately, while we have made great strides, today's search engines haven't reached that level of sophistication, so they have to engage in a guessing game, returning a smattering of the top choices that people have clicked on when they typed in "boston."

Once the search engine has matched a query to a set of documents, the next step is to return these results to the user. If the results set is small—less than ten documents—it's easy to display all of them on the first page. If the results set consists of hundreds, or thousands of possible matches, determining which ones to show first becomes a critical decision. This is a selection problem to which there is no single "best" answer because each searcher may have a different information need, even if the query is the same. Furthermore, because there are far too many matches for a common question like "boston history," the search engine must have guidelines for which of 272,000,000 matches to display first. For this purpose, search engines have developed a set of criteria for measuring relevance. The criteria evolve constantly as new information on user preferences and behavior is used to tune the engine.

Most Web search engines try to determine how much a document is about a topic. They have each developed a similar set of common sense criteria that they use to determine which documents to show first, but the differences in these criteria are responsible for differences in which documents show up on the first page. The criteria include:

- Number of times that the query terms show up in a document (term frequency), and how rare the term is in the collection (in other words, TF/IDF).

- How close together those terms appear in the document.

- Where the query terms appear in the document: title, first paragraph, topic headings in bold in the text?

- How important those terms are in differentiating one document from another: terms that are rare in the collection as a whole are given a higher weight.

- The number of links to the document from other sites on the Web.

- The relative value of links based on whether they are considered trustworthy and of high value. Sites that are highly respected, usually ".org" or ".edu" domains, or that are considered to be valuable because they are authoritative and point to and are pointed to often lend weight to a document's ranking.

- The number of times a link has been clicked on by other users who asked the same query.

- Non-document-based criteria such as which Web page the searcher is coming from, personal preferences, or search history, if these are available.

It makes sense that the more often a query term appears in a document, especially when that term appears in the title or section heading, the more likely it is to be about the query topic. It also makes sense that in multi-word queries, having the two terms appear within the same sentence would indicate that they are in some way related to each other in the document. That is a particularly important criterion, because many documents are about more than one topic. If we have a document about the cultural news of the week, it's possible to have "Boston" appear in the first paragraph about a new conductor for the Boston Symphony, and "history" appear three paragraphs later in a brief note about the founding of a new history museum in Oshkosh, Wisconsin.

In addition to establishing the "aboutness" of a document, it's also important to determine if that information is valuable and accurate. For this purpose, today's Web search engines use the Web as if it is a voting booth, examining which high value sites have selected a document to point to, and also tracking which documents are clicked on most often.

No discussion of relevance ranking on the Web would be complete without considering the financial aspects. Search engines are supported by advertising. They display links to pertinent advertisements at the top of their standard set of results. These links are paid for by advertisers who are hoping to attract traffic to their own sites. Advertisers bid a certain amount for each "click through" to their sites, and they certainly engage in a bidding war to attract that traffic. Search engines therefore have to balance the pertinence of the material on the advertiser's site with the amount that advertiser has bid for each click. The highest "relevant" bidder usually is displayed in those top three links, and advertisers engage in "search engine optimization" (SEO) to make sure that the material they display appears relevant according to the criteria above.

The decision for which document to display first has profound effects and some unexpected consequences. Searchers don't want to (and won't) wade through thousands of documents, so they rarely look at more than the first ten. Web sites, particularly eCommerce sites, must therefore jockey for position in the top ten results. Search position can mean the difference between a successful business and bankruptcy.

4.8.1   BEYOND THE DOCUMENT LIST

The previous section describes how basic search engines work. They return documents that are ranked by their relevance to a query, based primarily on the frequency with which the query terms appear in each document. However, as more and more information has arrived on the Web, helping searchers find answers, not just a list of documents, has become a priority. To ferret out clues to what a searcher may actually be interested in, Web search engines mine their query logs and their search histories to extract pertinent information and construct appropriate answers. This new approach to the search engine results page is a step toward becoming tomorrow's answer machines. One way that search engines have attacked the problem is to try to understand what *type* of question is being asked. They have created better answers for major recurring question types. For instance, suppose that my query is, "find flights to Boston from Seattle." The matching engine identifies the meaningful terms, like "Boston," "Seattle," and "flights." If the search engine has been designed to recognize frequent types of questions like "flights from A to B," then it resolves the ambiguity of city names by choosing the most likely "Boston," for instance, and then returns a list of flights rather than a document list, as the following screen shot from such a search on Microsoft's Bing shows (Figure 4.1). Note that

Bing has assembled the answer from multiple sources so that the searcher doesn't have to do this himself.

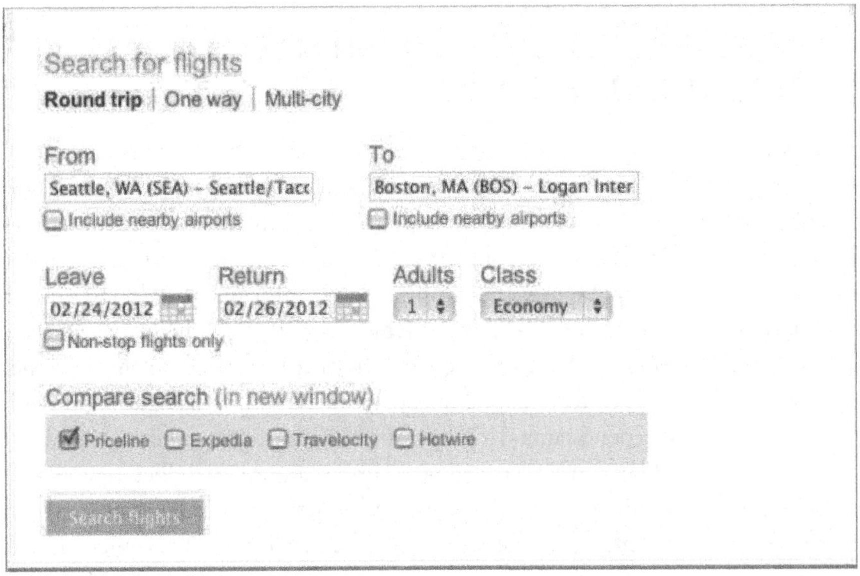

Figure 4.1: Search for flights.

These are early steps toward a real answer machine.

There are other ways of matching documents to queries instead of using the term frequency approach. One of the most powerful is probabilistic search. In this approach, the search engine is taught to recognize patterns of co-occurring words. This is one of the ways that humans remove the ambiguity of a term, by listening for the words that occur in conjunction with it. For instance, "car," when in the same context as words like steering wheel, drive train, automobile, etc., is probably about automobiles, while "car" in conjunction with "freight," "train," "rail," is probably about railroads. Of course, when a document about a collision of a train and an automobile occurs, it is difficult to determine which kind of "car" the document is about. In this approach, patterns are identified, usually with some sort of machine learning technology like naïve Bayes or a neural network. The system is trained on each category or subject with a set of documents that are selected as good examples of that topic. The system examines the training set of documents to find which patterns are common across all of them. It creates a model based on that pattern so that other documents that fit it will be categorized and disambiguated appropriately. The model must also be unique enough to differentiate that pattern from all the other subjects being indexed. At query time, the search engine predicts the probability that a document is about a topic based on how well each document represents the pattern for a category. It assigns a weight or value to each document returned depending on how certain it is that the query term is the central topic of the document. This score determines the relevance ranking of the document. Machine learning is used as well in some categorization, clustering, and question answering systems.

4.9   CATEGORIZATION, CLASSIFICATION, CLUSTERING, AND FACETED SEARCH

People categorize intuitively. Categories help us make sense of the world. They give us a consistent approach to handling similar events, people, or objects. Categorization and clustering technologies sort collections of information into meaningful groups of documents that are similar in some way. The grouping may be by topic, date, origin, author, access rights, archiving rules, or names of prominent people mentioned. These two approaches to organizing information add structure to a collection of information, and may reveal relationships among the groups. Both clustering and categorization are used to create browsing interfaces to a collection of information so that searchers can explore a collection without having to formulate a query. They aid online navigation and add metadata to documents in order to sharpen search. In other words, they improve the accessibility of a collection of information by creating pathways to groups of similar and related documents.

Clustering is an automatic approach that groups together similar documents and labels them with the major differentiating terms for each cluster. Clustering technologies identify features like similar word patterns and use those features to group documents together. Clustering must both group similar documents and differentiate between adjacent groups, so a clustering algorithm must also find which terms are key differentiators for each group, not just the most commonly occurring terms. Because the features are identified automatically, clustering the results of a search can be done immediately, creating an instant browsing interface for exploring a set of results. Clustering is also useful as a first step in developing more formal taxonomies.

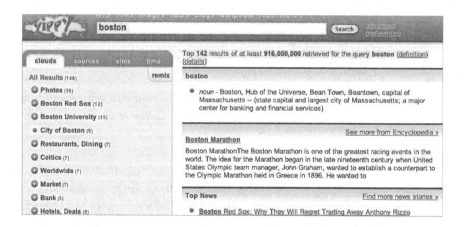

Figure 4.2: Search on Yippy for "Boston" with clustered results.

Figure 4.2 shows what a search for "Boston" looks like on Yippy, a Web clustering and search engine. Yippy performs a normal Web search, but then it clusters the results into meaningful groups that can be explored by clicking on each topic for further clusters. Because no taxonomy is necessary, the clustering works no matter what the query terms might be. The results are immediate, and make it possible for someone looking for information to either browse or search after the initial query. Exploration is often a preferred approach for searchers. Clustering provides immediate additional pathways into a collection of information.

Categorization, in contrast to clustering, groups together similar documents, objects, or events based on a predetermined formal view of a topic or collection, like a taxonomy or ontology. Like schemas in the structured world, categorization adds structure to a collection of information. A collection may have multiple taxonomies for different users (e.g., researchers, marketing managers, or sales people). Documents are either categorized using a set of rules for each node in the taxonomy, or, using machine learning, the system is given a training set of example documents for each topic in the taxonomy to help it create its own set of word patterns that represent the topic. For instance, a rule-based system might state that any document about the Boston Red Sox must contain the phrase "red sox" five or more times and also the terms "baseball" and "boston." A machine learning based system would be given a training set of documents about the Red Sox, and extract a pattern that required "red sox" to occur with three of the following: "sox," "baseball," "boston," "batter," "hits," and "base" within the same paragraph. Categorization can be entirely manual, entirely automatic (after the system is trained with examples), or a mixture of the two. Machine-aided categorization is a hybrid of automatic classification in which the system suggests terms that are confirmed or altered by human editors.

A partial taxonomy for Boston might look like Table 4.1.

Categorization can improve search when the categories, tags, or metadata are used to increase the weight of the major topics. Categorization can also remove the ambiguity of a term, disambiguating it into a single meaning because of the category it is in. Note that a topic can appear in more than one top category. Multiple pathways to the same information are one of the advantages of online systems.

Table 4.1: Partial Taxonomy for Boston

Events and Activities	Hotels and Food	Tourist Information
Sports	Hotels	Sightseeing
--Red Sox schedule and tickets	--By price	--Duck Boat Tours
--Patriots schedule and tickets	--By location	History
--Celtics schedule and tickets	Restaurants	Maps
Theater	--By name	Museums
Music	--By cuisine	Parks
--Fleet Center	--By location	Sports Teams
--Boston Symphony	Fast Food	-- Red Sox, etc.
--Boston Pops		Hazards
Shopping		--Boston Drivers
Festivals		Shopping
Events by date		Music and Theater
		(see also Events)

Browsing systems, including faceted search and directories, require clustering and categorization. Since categorization is based on sets of rules, there is no reason why those rules cannot be programmed into software in order to classify documents automatically. The caveat is that there are always exceptions, and that in dynamic worlds, topics often migrate, merge, or morph. Therefore, classification systems or taxonomies must be monitored closely and maintained regularly not only for accuracy but for usefulness. Once they impede, rather than improve access to knowledge, they must be changed.

There are a number of technologies used for categorization, including Support Vector Machines (SVM), neural networks, Naïve Bayes, K-Nearest Neighbor (KNN), as well as natural language processing, which uses defined rules that may include lists of synonyms and co-occurring terms. Each of these has its own strengths and weaknesses. For narrow collections in particular, in which the topics are all closely related, discriminating among them automatically is difficult. A good example of this type of collection would be the National Cancer Institute's, in which "cancer" is not a useful term to distinguish among documents. It's increasingly common for information access and management systems to use several categorizers in combination with each other in order to mitigate the weaknesses of any one system. Machine learning is discussed also in Chapter 6.

There are drawbacks to inaccurate categorization. Make categories too broad, and they will become a confusing hodgepodge. Conversely, if categories are too narrow, they may be too small to be useful. Categories, and the taxonomies they are based on, become outdated, so that knowledge managers must update them with new terminology. New categories may arise that must be added as the old ones become less useful. The consequences of miscategorization can be serious. Classify a mushroom as edible when it is toxic, and people may die. While the consequences of poor classification or taxonomy schemes are less dire in the information technologies, poorly thought-out taxonomies or schemas can hide materials from the people who need to find them. Frustration, botched decisions, and lost time are the results.

4.9.1 AUTOMATIC VS. MANUAL CATEGORIZATION

Most system administrators and knowledge workers are wary of automatic classification. They believe that nothing can rival humanly chosen subject headings. However, over fifty years of studies of professional indexers have demonstrated that humans are rarely consistent, even with themselves on different days. Because computers are consistent, even foolishly so, they churn out the same tag for the same pattern of words. They are unbiased, don't get tired, and don't need coffee breaks. The difference is that computers make dumb computer errors because all they can do is follow instructions. For instance, no human would categorize a document as positive that said, "I just love waiting in line—not," but a computer might. On the other hand, people are no more accurate, and they are certainly less consistent than computers. A person might consider a document to be about treatment of a disease one day, and about a clinical trial the next. People certainly make errors, but those errors make sense in a human context, so we tend to discount them.

4.10 NATURAL LANGUAGE PROCESSING (NLP) AND CONTENT ANALYTICS

Content analytics technologies and semantic search are based on natural language processing (NLP). NLP is a set of linguistically based techniques for determining the meaning of a word, a phrase, a sentence, or a document. *Text mining* or *text analytics* are terms for the same idea: that language is constructed from predictable rules and patterns, and that we can describe these patterns well enough to a computer so that it can process language the way humans do (with limitations). Content analytics is a broader term than text analytics that includes other forms of unstructured information like images, speech, or videos, as well as text. Whatever the term, the assumption is that if people can make sense of text or images that they haven't encountered before, we should be able to distill the rules that humans construct intuitively in order to describe them to a computer.

NLP research pursues the elusive question of how we understand the meaning of a sentence or a document. What are the clues we use to understand who did what to whom, or when something happened? What is fact and what is opinion or prediction? Words are the basic building blocks of meaning in any language. In addition to their dictionary meaning, words perform a role (subject, verb, object, modifier) within a sentence that describes the relationship of one word to another. We rely on both the semantic meaning and syntax to determine the true meaning of a text.

People extract meaning from text or spoken language on several levels. In order to understand natural language processing (NLP), it is important to be able to distinguish among these, since not all "NLP" systems use every level. These levels are:

1. **Phones and phonemes** describe the way words are pronounced in spoken language. This level is not important for written text in information retrieval systems. However, variations in pronunciation can trip up people who are trying to understand spoken language and it is a real problem for voice recognition systems that must understand regional differences as well as non-native speakers trying to speak another language. I will never forget my freshman roommate from Brooklyn rattling on about the great play by a guy named "Shore" she was reading in English class. "I never heard of him," I said. She answered incredulously, "You never heard of George Bernard Shore [Shaw]?" To unite variants in pronunciation, we normalize spoken words to the *phonemic* level that represents all common variants in the same way.

2. **Morphology**. The morpheme is the smallest piece of a word that carries meaning. Examples are word stems like *child* (*childlike, childish, children* are all built on this stem) or prefixes and suffixes like *un-* , or *–ation*, or *–s* for plural. Many search engines are able to determine word stems on a rudimentary level. This usually means that they can automatically offer you both the singular and plural form of a word, which is a nice feature. Automatic use of morphology without accompanying understanding, however, can also return some pretty funny documents. In the early days of search engines, they would stem a word like "*communication*" and return *community, commune, communication*, or *communism*.

3. **Syntax**. When we parsed a sentence in grade school, we were identifying the role that each word played in it, and that word's relationships to the other words in the sentence. Position in a sentence can determine whether a word is the subject or the object of an action. *Fred hit John* and *John hit Fred* both use the same words, but the meaning is quite different, particularly to the person who is the object of the verb *hit*.

NLP systems, in their fullest implementation, use syntactic structure to answer questions like "Which company bought Autonomy?" correctly. Hewlett Packard is the right and only answer to this question, but without the syntactic information, a search engine would look for instances of "acquire" or "buy" and return the long list of companies that Autonomy had bought. This kind of information is invaluable in finding out side effects of drugs, discovering disease vectors, or relationships among terrorists and drug lords. It is used in good online question answering systems for online self-help that have become prevalent on manufacturers' web sites. When this additional information is stored, it makes it possible to ask, "Who dropped the golden apple for Atlanta?" without retrieving reams of information about apples in the city of Atlanta.

The structure of a sentence conveys meanings and relationships between words even if we don't know what they mean. In this excerpt from "The Jabberwocky" by Lewis Carroll, the words that usually carry meaning—the nouns, verbs, adjectives, and adverbs are all nonsense words. Nevertheless, we get a glimmer of meaning because of the syntax and the words that are usually structural, like articles, prepositions, and conjunctions:

Twas brillig, and the slithy toves
Did gyre and gimble in the wabe:

All mimsy were the borogoves,
And the mome raths outgrabe.

In this sentence, we know that the scene that is described happened in the past (Twas). *Brillig* is probably an adjective, perhaps describing the weather. We know that *slithy* is an adjective describing toves, which is a plural noun. All this meaning is conveyed by the syntax of the sentence. It fits the same sentence template as "It was windy in the silent city."

4. **Semantics**. The semantic level examines words for their *dictionary meaning* and for the meaning that they have within the context of a sentence. Semantics recognizes that most words have more than one meaning but that we can resolve the ambiguity of a word and choose the most appropriate meaning by looking at the rest of the sentence. The charm of the Amelia Bedelia books by Peggy Parish comes from Amelia Bedelia confusing the *senses* of a word (draw the drapes, dress the chicken, dust the furniture, put out the lights).

It takes both syntax and semantics to pin down meaning. Let's look at our Lewis Carroll example again. The Jabberwocky makes sense at the syntactic level. It has some major problems at the semantic level. At the semantic level, we can finally ask what do *brillig, slithy,* and *toves* mean. We found quite a bit of meaning in that sentence on the syntactic level, but it fails completely at the semantic level.

Context determines which sense to assign to the verb *to draw* in *"He drew his snickersnee"* (*The Mikado*, Gilbert and Sullivan). Even if we don't know what a snickersnee is, the fact that the rest of the song is about an execution determines that the character, Ko-Ko, is talking about drawing a sword of some sort, not an artistic activity. Some meaning is entirely dependent on context. For instance, if a document is discussing how to enter data in a table then "the table" probably doesn't refer to a hardwood dining room table.

Phrase identification, which is partly semantics, partly syntax, is particularly important for identifying the meaning of a word. For example, in English, precise meaning is often carried by noun phrases—two nouns that together mean something quite different from their constituent words. Using an appropriate noun phrase is an excellent technique for searching any retrieval system. NLP can automatically identify phrases such as *box office, carbon copy, dress circle, walking stick,* or *blind date*.

5. **Discourse level**. This level examines the structure of a document and uses this large structure to extract additional meaning. Some of the structural elements might be headings, or the chapters of a book. Document types differ depending on their purpose—research, news, or story. For instance, a newspaper article typically reports the most important facts—who—what—when—where—why—how—at the beginning, usually in the first paragraph. In contrast, a mystery novel never tells you who did it and how it was done until the end. A technical document starts with an abstract, summarizes the document in a single paragraph, and then enlarges on all these points in the body of the work. NLP uses this predictable structure "to

understand what the specific role of a piece of information is in a document, for example—is this a conclusion, is this an opinion, is this a prediction, or is this a fact?" (Liddy)

6. **Pragmatic level**. The practical or pragmatic level of understanding relies on a body of knowledge about the world that is derived from sources outside the document. For example, we know that France, Germany, Belgium, Spain, etc. are in Europe. We can either add a list of all the cities, states, and countries in a region to a query ourselves, or we can use knowledge bases to help the system automatically expand a query to all of these localities. It's much easier to let the system do the work if we want to find the effects of the euro on European economies. Many retrieval systems can embed lists of synonyms, names of products and people, taxonomies and ontologies in order to expand and improve relevance and recall.

Although we have discussed these levels of understanding as if they were independent, in fact, they are intertwined. The role of the word within the structure of a sentence narrows the choice of reasonable meanings. A combination of context and syntax determine what "plant" means in the sentence, "I watered the plant as soon as I got back to the house." We know that it isn't reasonable to assume that "plant" is a verb in this sentence, since it is the object of the verb "to water." That is context-independent. However, within the context of this sentence we can narrow the meaning still further, since it is unlikely that the speaker carried home an industrial plant, or that she would water it when she got it there.

Each of these levels of language understanding follows definable patterns or rules that can be coded for computer understanding. Nevertheless, humans delight in breaking those rules, and the problem has only gotten worse as we have added new channels of communication like Twitter or Facebook, with their own unique syntactic and semantic elements. One of the greatest challenges for NLP systems is to distill a sentence, sentence fragment, or document down to an absolutely precise, unambiguous representation of its contents. Computers, after all, are not human, and they will do only what they are told to do. They do not make flying leaps of understanding based on skimpy evidence, so they do not deal well with ambiguity or word-play.

4.11   TIME, SENTIMENT, AND GEO-LOCATION

In addition to analyzing text for its semantic and syntactic meanings, NLP systems can also extract specialized terms for time, for feelings or opinions (sentiment), and for geographic location.

Text is full of phrases that indicate time. Some are unambiguous: *January 17th 1980 at 8AM* or *March 6th 1977 at 2PM*. Others are relative: *today, tomorrow,* or *yesterday* all depend on when I am writing. The same applies to geographic location: *15 Maple Ave., Niagara Falls* is a definite location that can be placed on a map. But *five blocks south of where you are standing with your iPhone* is a relative statement of location. Nevertheless, with some help, like knowing where Niagara Falls is or when a document is being written, the time statements can all be placed on a timeline and the geographic statements can all be placed on a map.

Sentiment, in contrast, is highly subjective, and difficult to pin down. Especially in informal social settings like Facebook or Twitter, word usage can be ambiguous and perverse. For instance, "*wicked good performance*" is a likely tweet from a Bostonian that uses two words—*wicked* and *good*—that are usually considered opposites. In this regional usage, though, wicked intensifies good. Nevertheless, understanding whether someone is pleased or angry is a hot area of software development today. Tracking what one's customers are saying about a product, and whether they are pleased or annoyed by it has become a big business. Today, businesses invest in sentiment software to monitor how their brands are performing in the marketplace, and also to defuse angry customers by contacting them with help and advice.

Geographic location can be extracted from text so that phrases like, "on Edgell Rd., at the Sudbury-Framingham line," can be plotted on a map. This use combines text analytics with geospatial knowledge bases so that the location described in the text can be translated to geographic coordinates.

4.12 NLP IN INFORMATION RETRIEVAL

NLP improves information retrieval at several points in the process from document ingestion to analysis. By adding metadata to documents, NLP removes ambiguity and sharpens search. NLP can expand queries by adding synonyms. It can create a dialog with the user to improve a query before the system returns results. And, NLP provides the analytics and browsing interfaces that have begun to turn the black box of search into an interactive information environment. While NLP is not a necessity in information retrieval, systems that use more NLP, and at more levels of language understanding have the most potential for building the data mining and advanced information retrieval systems of the future.

Full NLP interprets and stores meaning at all stages and at all levels for both the query and the document. As in any computer system, the choice of how much NLP is necessary is based on practical considerations. NLP requires longer ingestion processes, and results in larger search indexes because of the additional metadata. Questions to consider might include how computationally expensive the additional processing will be. Or do the predicted uses of the search results require the extra processing and the larger index size? Will it slow down the processing of queries unacceptably? How much overhead does it add to document processing? Are the retrieved results so much better that the additional costs are worth the trade-off? Question answering systems need deep NLP to return accurate intelligent answers, but applications that look for trends may only need entity extraction and/or sentiment extraction.

Many systems that boast that they use "semantic search" are actually using shallow, rather than deep NLP—for extracting phrases and proper nouns, or by using co-occurring terms to disambiguate queries. Some may suggest better queries by using their query logs to suggest related phrases and synonyms. Just adding these features, however, improves the accuracy of search results.

The search and analytics systems that use deep NLP today tend to be confined to specialized applications like question answering for call centers or online self-help systems. However, full document and query processing on all levels of language understanding is usually a requirement for text analytics in Voice of the Customer (sentiment monitoring) applications and when text analytics is incorporated into a full business intelligence suite. To mine text for sentiment and opinion, or to discover patterns and relationships like the side effects of drugs, or for competitive intelligence and real decision support, full NLP is a requirement.

4.12.1   SOME COMMON USES OF NLP

Document categorization and tagging

This area has the most promise for new improvements to information access systems and for business analytics. At this stage information is extracted and stored about each document. Retrieval systems can only retrieve what they contain. The more extensively analyzed the content is, the more potential the knowledge base has for use with future, more intelligent systems. If we can extract and store a rich collection of data, even if we don't use that data immediately, we have created a strong foundation for future applications as they arrive. Knowledge bases can be used today to expand queries with synonyms, to increase accuracy through extracted names of people, places, and things, and to provide browsing access to collections. Unified information access systems are already using content analytics to tag database collections as well as text. Question answering systems also depend on having this deep analysis of text if they are to return smart answers.

Query interpretation and matching

There are two obvious advantages to using NLP at this stage. The first is that it is much easier to convey our information need including intention and meaning if we can use the full power of real language. Speaking in code is difficult, and it leaves out important aspects of thought. The second is that use of full NLP can eliminate problems that plague us such as false drops and other right word/wrong meaning retrievals. False drops are documents that are returned that contain the search term, but with the wrong meaning of the word. For instance, a search for *phone* might return the linguistic meaning for phone—a phonetic sound—instead of information on telephones and cell phones. NLP can focus a query without eliminating potentially useful documents. It should improve both recall and precision. NLP can also expand a query to add synonyms and alternate forms as well as related geographic terms.

Document ranking

NLP can improve the ranking of documents because it has done a better job of matching the meaning and the intention of both the document and the query. It has more evidence of what is really relevant on which to base a relevance judgment.

Text analytics for unified information access

Unified information access platforms unite access to multiple structured and unstructured information sources. Text analytics technologies are used in several places in unified information access: to categorize and tag documents at ingestion, to create browsing interfaces, and to interpret queries more precisely. Unified information access platforms use text analytics to discover similar concepts across structured databases and unstructured text, even if they are expressed differently. We will discuss unified access in more detail in Chapter 5.

Text analytics for business intelligence

Business intelligence applications are well established. They come with well-accepted reporting and visualization tools and they have garnered an audience of trained business analysts. What they don't have is access to the roughly 85% of information that is not structured. This means that they can report on what is happening, where it is happening, and who is doing it, but they can't report on why it's happening. The reason is that cause and effect are often buried in reams of text that can't be mined by standard business intelligence applications. Technicians write notes about what they observe when they repair a car. Physicians write notes about their patients, but rarely have check-off codes that accurately reflect what they actually see. Customers write emails or call the service desk with problems that are described well in text but don't fit in the neat boxes on the medical, repair, or insurance forms.

Text analytics, however, can extract cause and effect, relationships and patterns, sentiment, time, location, or statements of fact that can be mined once they are integrated into business analytics applications. Marrying the two gives analysts a full picture of an event or a trend. For instance, when a timeline of stock trades was matched with news reports about various stocks, it was possible to find evidence of insider trading: if trading increased after company news was released, then changes in trading activity made sense, but if it occurred before the news was public, then insiders were using their knowledge to get a jump on the market.

Text analytics is also used today to improve predictive models. In one example, text analytics extracted the pattern of key phrases that customers who were about to abandon their mobile carrier used in their calls with customer service. The pattern of usage differed from that of disgruntled customers who were not likely to move to a new carrier. Knowing that, the original carrier was able to identify the customers most likely to jump ship and offer them a better deal.

Text analytics in advertising

Text analytics is used to deliver more appropriate ads to users. Better interpretation of both the query and the advertisement improves the relevance of ad to query, and should increase the click through rate, as well as user satisfaction.

Text analytics for Visualization

Visualization represents categories, facets, or relationships in a concise, visual manner, often using graphs and charts, so that users can understand a collection of information quickly. For instance, faceted search (see Daniel Tunkelang's book, "Faceted Search") uses categories and entities that have been extracted from a collection of text in order to guide the user to either topics or products of interest. Dosage and side effects that have been extracted from medical articles are shown in the screen shot from Linguamatics, Figure 4.3.

4.13   MULTILINGUAL AND CROSS LANGUAGE SEARCH, GISTING, AND TRANSLATION

It should be apparent by now that search depends on language—the words and grammatical structures that make up each language. While any search engine can match a string of letters or Chinese characters in a query to the same string in a document, understanding what the string means, or even if it is part of a larger word is not easy without specialized tools that are specific to each language: language identifiers, tokenizers to identify word boundaries, dictionaries, lists of synonyms, and even industry-specific word lists. Most software research and development, as well as most Web sites, have focused on English speakers. However, for 70% of Internet users, English is not their native language. Studies show that online buyers will not buy as often from Web sites that are not in their native language. Furthermore, as research and development have burgeoned around the world, researchers need to find research reports that are pertinent to their areas of study, no matter what language they are written in. It's important, as a matter of both relationships and revenue, to enable native speakers of one language to operate in other language environments. There are a number of approaches to solving these problems.

Cross language and multilingual search translates queries into the target language in order to find pertinent documents. The query translation is usually based on cross language dictionaries or collections of translated text in multiple languages, called "parallel corpora," that suggest appropriate terms based on the original query. Results are returned either in the original languages, or with a gist or machine translation to help the searcher figure out what the "gist" of the document is. In the screen shot below (Figure 4.4), the searcher can enter a search in English, and see the results from other languages, as well as a preview of the original document. Names are identified in multiple languages, and the facets on the left allow browsing by language, by person's name, or location.

Gisting applications also use knowledge bases like cross language dictionaries, semantic networks that have collected words on the same topic in a single node of the network, or parallel corpora like WordNet in multiple languages. For a document in a foreign language, gists typically return a list of concepts and possibly proper nouns that help the searcher decide whether or not a document is of interest.

Machine translation software translates text from one language to another. While it can certainly substitute a French word, for instance, for its English language equivalent, the results are far from satisfying and sometimes hilarious. Today, machine translation software takes advantage of the massive polyglot information on the Web to create parallel corpora that boost the accuracy of translation by examining the same topic in multiple languages. As the translation system is used, it learns from criticism and mistakes and incorporates that knowledge into the system to improve its accuracy. Machine translations today are good enough for real time chat, for eCommerce questions, for customer support, and for researchers who want to read a document in their field without the

Pharmacologic Substance	Safety issues	Tissue	Dosage	Doc	Hit
Cyclosporine	Safety issues	Kidney	15 mg/kg/day	22 17497475	... of hyperbaric oxygen on cyclosporine-induced nephrotoxicity and oxidative stress in rats.... a control group, a cyclosporine group (15 mg/kg/day intraperitoneally for 14 days).
Mycophenolate Moietl	Safety issues	Kidney	2 g/day	4 16152998	7 Uncommon site effect of MMF in renal transplant recipients... Patients used MMF 2 g/day.
Amphotericin B	Safety issues	Kidney	0.4 mg/kg/day	2 15761070	8 Low nephrotoxicity of an effective amphotericin B... for 10 consecutive days with 0.4 mg/kg/day AMB in the form of traditional...
Everolimus	Safety issues	Kidney	1.5 mg/day	3 16041270	3 Concerns over nephrotoxicity led to a protocol amendment... kiss to follow-up) were everolimus 1.5 mg/day, 33.7% (65)...
Gentamicin	Safety issues	Kidney	100 mg/kg/day	2 14748758	6 ...4-hydroxy tempo) on gentamicin-induced nephrotoxicity in rats.... The rats were given gentamicin (100 mg/kg/day i.p., once a ...
Alcohol	Safety issues	Liver	20 g/day	1 15553597	7 Insulin sensitivity and hepatic steatosis in obese subjects with ... analyzed 86 obese patients whose alcohol intake was less than 20 g/day and who showed no signs...
Lamivudine	Safety issues	Liver	100 mg/day	5 17283489	1 Lamivudine (100 mg/day) was continued throughout the ..... Liver Transplantation adverse effects
Sirolimus	Safety issues	Kidney	1 mg/day	2 16364861	2 ... primary immunosuppressant in calcineurin inhibitor-induced nephrotoxicity... Sirolimus was started at 1 mg/day with titration over 2 weeks ....
		Liver	2 mg/day	1 15899725	1... of sirolimus, participants received sirolimus 2 mg/day for at least 7 days... dropped out because of trimethoprim-sulfamethoxazole-related hepatotoxicity.
Atorvastatin	Safety issues	Liver	10mg/day	3 17473378	3 ... a potential role in statin-related adverse events, and withdrawal of ... in patients developing myotoxicity of liver toxicity... Twenty-six patients with hypercholesterolemia received atorvastatin at 10 mg/day for 3 months.
			80mg/day	1 16731999	1... that intensive lipid-lowering therapy with atorvastatin 80 mg/day provides significant clinical benefit beyond ... in the rates of treatment-related adverse events and persistent elevations in liver enzymes.
		Kidney	10mg/d	2 17889157	2 ...) were treated posttransplantation with atorvastatin (10 mg/d) for 12 weeks without ... Kidney Transplantation adverse effects immunology physiology

Compound

Potential safety issues

In this organ

At this dosage

Figure 4.3: Linguamatics. Used with permission of Linguamatics. © Linguamatics 2012.

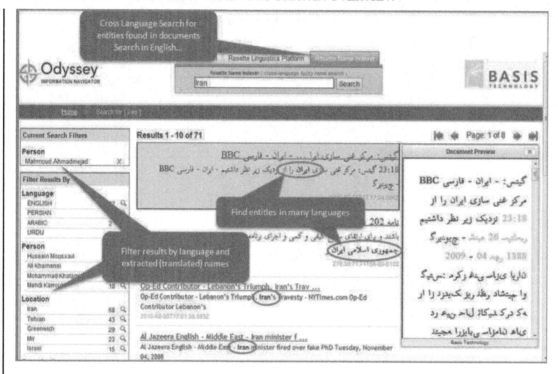

Figure 4.4: Odyssey.

delay or expense of hiring a translator. When translations require literary elegance, the human touch is still necessary.

4.14   KNOWLEDGE BASES

Out of the box, search and content analytics do a decent job, but to improve their accuracy, they need additional tools. Clustering and categorization help, but vendors tell us that adding specialized collections of knowledge to the system can boost accuracy from the 60-70% that is considered a reasonable baseline to up to 80-90% or more... This is akin to having an astrophysicist answer a question on black holes instead of someone with a 9th grade earth science background. Expertise matters.

Most enterprise search engines provide tools for adding corporate knowledge bases such as lists of product names and personnel, as well as useful internal terminology. They also come with tools for importing, building, or modifying taxonomies. Many with NLP features include WordNet in one or more languages. WordNet is a hierarchical database of terms, their synonyms, and their relationships to each other. For instance, in the example below, a dog is a type of animal, and collies and Labrador retrievers types of dogs; a cat is also an animal, and lions, tigers, and Siamese cats are all subtypes of cats.

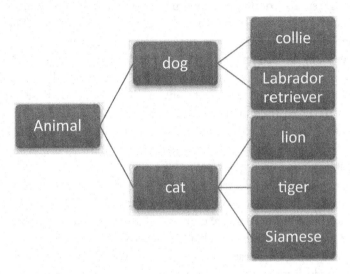

WordNet exists in multiple languages, making it possible to map terms for the same concept from one language to another. Commonly used knowledge bases in addition to WordNet include industry-specific taxonomies (e.g., automobile manufacturing, oil and gas, electronics, clothing, and other consumer goods), dictionaries, and parallel corpora like translation memories that are specific to an organization and its products and services.

4.14.1 RICH MEDIA SEARCH

Sounds and images are great bearers of meaning, but compared to text, that meaning is several orders of magnitude more difficult to define for retrieval. Rich media retrieval depends on the same types of technologies as text retrieval for finding files that match a query: extraction of meaningful elements, indexing, similarity matching, categorization, machine learning, relevance ranking, and specialized interfaces to present the results to the user. However, with image and video search, it is especially challenging to determine which elements are meaningful. In a picture of two people on a beach at sunset, is the sunset important? Should we categorize the image for romance? For happiness? For vacations?

This book concentrates on text retrieval and analytics. However, rich media search—of speech, music, images and video files—is a closely related area of development. At first, rich media files were retrieved using textual metadata tags for elements like title, names of speakers or performers, topic, date, location, author, producer, composer, etc. This is still the method used for the majority of rich media retrieval systems, but tagging images and videos manually has become an overwhelming task. However, there are a number of technologies that have been developed to retrieve these media directly. Speech recognition is the furthest along, and authoring tools that understand the spoken word and translate it to text have been on the market for some time. These may either be trained to the voice of a single speaker, or they may recognize sounds using phonetic and phonemic dictionaries. For instance, speech recognition is used for closed captioning in television. The results are not perfect, but they are adequate to give viewers the gist of what is being said.

Like speech, music also has discrete elements that can be extracted. Notes, rhythm, key signature, instruments or voices, and patterns of chord sequences are all identifiable. In fact, there are search engines today that allow the user to hum a tune so that the search engine can find similar songs. Also, just as it's possible for a musician to suspect that an unfamiliar work is by Beethoven, search engines that have been trained on Beethoven examples can identify him as the most likely composer, based on the similarity of chord and rhythm patterns. This technology is still somewhat experimental, and is in use on popular music Web sites.

Images present additional challenges because identifying meaningful elements is not easy. Pixels alone won't tell you whose face appears in an image. And dogs, horses, elephants and tables all have four legs. Because the language of images is abstract once we get beyond colors and shapes, the form of the query is a problem as well. How do we submit a query for a romantic evening? If we ask for "romantic evening on a beach at sunset" today, we will retrieve images that have been tagged with those key words. But what about using an image as a query? Can we point to a picture and ask for others like it? How does a visual search engine identify the salient elements in an image without text tags? At present, manual tagging is the state of the art, and sites like Flickr have popularized photo sharing and tagging to develop large archives of tagged images. Visual search engines must be iterative and adaptive if they are to define what the user is really looking for. Because of the complexity of the content, image retrieval systems must rely on multiple technologies and sources of evidence: collections of tagged images, systems trained to recognize standard objects, fuzzy matching, categorization and machine learning, and adaptive interfaces that invite browsing and interaction.

Table 4.2: *Continues.*

Summary: Search and Discovery Technologies and Uses

Technology	Definition	Uses
Categorization and Classification	Groups together documents about the same topic according to predetermined categories, often derived from a taxonomy or ontology.	Sharpens search by determining "aboutness." Disambiguates terms. Enables browsing and exploration of text collections and search results sets.
Clustering	Groups documents by similarity based on occurrence of similar terms in the documents and the dissimilarity of each cluster to other documents in a collection.	Quick browsing of collections and search results without the need for predetermined categories. Useful for discovering new topics that might not appear in formal taxonomies.
Connectors	Connect search and other systems to information sources—file servers, Web sites, databases.	Enable search systems to gather and index data from multiple sources or to distribute queries to other sources and information systems.
Entity extraction	Identifies names of people, places, things (proper nouns, noun phrases, specialized terms like names of chemicals, product names).	Browsing, Content analytics, auto tagging, business intelligence, unified access, master data management. Extracts facets for faceted navigation and to enrich search index by adding terms. Also used to structure text for business analytics.
Exact match	Delivers exact matches to a query.	Useful for known item searches, database searches, searches that return too many results.
Fuzzy match	Matches query terms to documents, delivers both exact and near or approximate matches to a query. Matches the query approximately in spelling, in number of terms matched.	Relaxes the strictures of an exact match query, finding additional relevant documents that may be pertinent. Useful for cleaning up database duplicates, as well as for information retrieval.
Index	The inverted index is an index of all the terms and all their locations in all of the documents in a collection.	Basic search engine architecture.
Part of speech tagging	Parses sentences. Tags each word for part of speech and function in sentence: e.g.: noun/subject; verb; noun phrase; noun/object.	Finds phrases to sharpen search. Disambiguates terms. Used for relationship extraction.

Table 4.3: *Continued.*		
Relationship extraction	Identifies, extracts, and stores relationships between entities. Also known as "triples," or fact or event extraction. A triple consists of the noun, verb, and object in a sentence: the actor, the action, and who or what was acted upon (e.g., Bob hit Bill vs. Bill hit Bob.)	Triples provide direct answers to questions like "who bought YouTube?" Finds relationships such as cause and effect,acquisitions and mergers, relationship between terrorists and criminals. Used in question answering systems, online self-help systems, business intelligence and data mining.
Relevance ranking	Ranks documents that match a query by a set of criteria such as frequency of occurrence of the query term in a document. Documents are presented in decreasing probability that they are a good match to a query.	Relevance ranking is used to display the best or closest matches to a query first, followed by those that match the query less closely. Users need relevance ranking to find the best documents quickly so that they don't have to sort through too many results.
Search engine	Matches queries to documents in the index. Returns documents that match query terms or concepts.	Retrieves pertinent documents, displays citations for browsing based on interaction design criteria.
Sentiment extraction	Identifies whether an opinion about an entity or event is positive, negative or neutral.	Voice of the customer, call center, market intelligence, advanced trading applications, politics, and more.
Taxonomies and other knowledge bases	Organized guides to a topic, often hierarchical. Shows topics in a collection and their relationships to each other.	Used for categorization, browsing, automated document processing, faceted navigation.
Time extraction	Identifies the time that an event occurred/ Extracts both relative and specific terms relating to time: e.g., "yesterday" or 3/21/64.	Used to create timelines, re-create order in which actions or events occurred, track trends, create heat maps.
Tokenization	Determines word boundaries.	Necessary first step in parsing text for indexing or content analytics.
Visualization	Represents information graphically for purposes of information interaction and exploration.	Interactive information access, particularly to large collections of information. Browsing and faceted navigation interfaces. Bar and timeline charts showing trends, comparing positive and negative sentiment on a product. Maps for store locations, or emergency management.

CHAPTER 5

Information Access: A Spectrum of Needs and Uses

Search and discovery technologies satisfy a spectrum of information needs in information seeking, information organization, management, and analysis. These technologies are related in that they try to make sense of language so that a computer can perform some of the information gathering and analysis tasks that come naturally to people. By extension, these technologies are also useful in finding, analyzing, or organizing digital images, speech, or music, which have many of the same qualities as text: subjective content that needs a degree of latitude or fuzziness in order to identify similarities among records.

In this spectrum of uses, however, technologies are only one of the necessary elements to consider. The users, the tasks they are engaged in, the form of answers needed, the types and formats of the information to be searched, organized, and analyzed, and the interaction design all determine the best combination of technologies for a specific task. For that reason, it's important to understand each of these parameters as a first step in selecting search technology. This chapter discusses types of information tasks, users, and answers, as well as some examples that demonstrate the intersection of users, task, design, and technology. Included are some of the variables to consider in defining what the right search application might be, and the trade-offs that are necessary in designing a search system.

5.1 INFORMATION TASKS

We lump all kinds of information finding tasks under the rubric "search," but each of the following information tasks requires a different combination of technologies and interaction design. Some common information seeking tasks are:

- Find a "known item." Locate a document that you already know exists but can't find, e.g., "Find the slide I created last month on big data, not the one I did three months ago." The user knows what she is looking for, but it's buried among fifty presentations on the same topic on her desktop. There is only one right answer. An interface that shows a preview of the closest matches saves the user having to open one document after another to find the right one.

- Gather a broad collection about a topic. Broad searches must find a good sampling of information about a topic from multiple sources and viewpoints. The answer should be a representative collection of good documents about all aspects. Tangentially related information is welcome as it may spur new ideas. These searches may return massive amounts of information that must be presented with tools for exploring the collection easily. A user interface that allows exploration through faceted browsing, clustering, or categorization, as well as suggested related terms makes this a much easier task.

- Find everything about a topic but nothing that is extraneous to it. Patent searching and eDiscovery are both good examples of this. The answer should include every pertinent document in a collection, but omit anything that is tangentially related or not related at all. The goal is to create a narrowly defined, highly relevant collection.

- Find an expert on a topic. Many organizations index their staff so that they can find them when they need to locate a knowledgeable expert to answer a question or work on a project.

- Browse a collection of information to see what's there. Browsing answers the question "what's here?" and is a valuable alternative to search. It requires a logical organization, often a hierarchy of broad to narrow topics that guides a searcher to documents or answers. Browsing lets you wander through a collection of information to get a sense of its contents and layout. Browsing helps users locate information when they have trouble formulating a query. Multiple pathways through the collection that lead to an information nugget are useful, since searchers may approach a topic from different angles.

- Explore and analyze an information space. These complex iterative processes explore a collection of information, looking for categories, entities, and relationships among the information elements. They require tools to slice, dice, and rearrange information elements, looking for relationships, trends, social graphs, and networks. The tools must allow the user to interact with the collection visually, narrowing down a topic, moving to an adjacent topic, querying, browsing, analyzing, charting, and visualizing the collection from multiple angles. Search and discovery for research and innovation is an extreme example of broad topic search mixed with exploration and analysis of an information space. The process of innovation is an iterative one, starting with extensive information gathering to spur the thinking process. Serendipity is a necessary ingredient because the true innovator operates in the interstices between domains. Bringing together physics and biology or economics and complexity theory requires an open mind, broad knowledge and curiosity, a problem to solve, and time to think. We are only beginning to figure out how to design systems that can support the innovation process, but we do know that innovators look for new angles and ideas that will jog them into an "aha moment." These systems must offer unexpected, but valuable connections to the researcher. Quite a challenge.

- Answer a question. Question answering systems return answers, not lists of documents. Questions like, how do I fix my faucet, identify a deer tick, build a gazebo, bone a fish, or put a picture on my Web site, are asking for help, not pointers to a list of possible sources. Question answering systems return answers in whatever format is most appropriate: charts, graphs, videos, or even a phone call from a customer service representative. Online self-help systems are good examples of this kind of system.

- Monitor a stream of information and alert the user when something new arrives or when a change such as an increase or decrease in information volume occurs in the stream. Alerting for new job postings on a competitor's site is a good example of this type of activity.

- Search by defined attributes. Also called parametric search, this is a specialized interface for finding information about products or topics according to various attributes of the items. For instance, a flower identification site might display the features to look for in identifying a flower such as color, number of petals, types of leaves, etc. This type of interface is "query-less," in the sense that when a user clicks on a set of attributes, the system can construct a query without the user overtly entering it. Parametric search helps users explore an information space and understand how it is organized. It frames a query that is appropriate for the system. The system can be designed so that it doesn't offer any choices for which there are no results. In other words, selecting one category limits the choices offered in succeeding steps.

- eCommerce often uses parametric search and is a specialized kind of search that includes search and browsing within a commercial context. For instance, an online shoe retailer might display shoes by:

  - Ladies, men's, or children's shoes
  - Size
  - Type of shoe: dress, casual, hiking, sandals
  - Color

If you are planning a vacation or buying a new sound system, integrating search and browse with recommendations, expert reviews, peer reviews, discussion forums, and secure purchasing tools is an online necessity. The purpose is to connect potential buyers with the right product, rather than queries with the best answer. Because eCommerce includes other considerations besides finding the best matching document, questions of what's in stock, whether a product is recommended and by whom, price, size, and the need for images of the product mandate that this specialized type of search environment include rules engines, databases, social forums, publishing features, recommendation engines, search engine optimization, and a number of other tools. See also Section 5.5.2, eCommerce Search.

- Find relationships among people, places, things, or events that are described in a collection of information. Some of these relationships might be:

  - Cause and effect: people taking drug X developed indigestion when it was taken simultaneously with drug Y.
  - Mergers and acquisitions: company A bought company B for $Z millions.

  - Crime and terrorism: relationship of crime syndicates to terrorist groups is shown through pattern of email messages and funds transfers.

• Find patterns and trends in large and constantly changing sets of data. Some examples of this kind of information task include finding:

  - Growing investment trend in copper indicates need to hop on the bandwagon early to benefit from rising stock prices

  - Customer dissatisfaction due to squeaky suspension in new automobile

  - Fraud: false healthcare coverage claims can be tied to a small number of addresses

  - Customer churn: customers who demand a new phone "asap" are likely to switch to another carrier unless they are given a better subscription deal

  - Epidemics: increase in local media coverage foreshadows spread of flu that can be tracked geographically as it moves from one region to the next

  - Hospital readmissions: unexpected congestive heart failure indicators can be tied to likelihood of readmission to the hospital

  - Successful sales practices: finds sales activities that are tied to unusually good or poor performance

• Discover patterns to use in building models for predictive modeling. For this use, the searcher must gather and analyze data, often from a large collection of mixed formats and data types. The patterns are used to create scenarios on which to base decisions for handling a perceived trend. The results of the information gathering must be consumed by typical predictive modeling and BI tools, so formatting the output is critical. Examples of this kind of usage include:

  - When to intervene in care of patient who seems likely to be readmitted to hospital, and what the most effective intervention might be

  - When to invest in a stock market trend and when to pull funds out of the market

  - When to initiate extreme steps (e.g., quarantine, travel restrictions) to contain a burgeoning epidemic, and what the effects of those steps might be on health vs. the economic welfare of a community

  - When to contact disgruntled customers to rectify problems with cars or other products they have purchased. What the benefit of that intervention might be (retain customers, improve reputation in the marketplace) vs. the cost of time and repairs

5.2   INFORMATION SEEKERS

Users of information systems come in all shapes, sizes, interests, and backgrounds. Designing for the occasional searcher as well as for the searcher with a three-hour-a-day searching habit is not easy. Salespeople, marketing professionals, researchers, leisure searchers, customers, and suppliers all have different information needs and tasks to accomplish. Today's enterprise search systems and Web search engines are generic, and they rarely fit these very different requirements. That is changing, however, as search systems learn more about individuals, the role they play within their organizations, or their search history if they are using a Web engine. This is a double-edged sword, since it feels "creepy" to have a piece of machinery know that you bought a cookbook for your mother three months ago. Or worse, lets you know that it has already found all of your friends on Facebook and is using them to guess at your interests. No one has managed to strike the right balance between good personalized search and invasion of privacy. Within the organization, in the United States, it is perfectly permissible to collect information on whatever an employee is doing during work time. On the Web, the dividing line is murkier. "Opt-in" policies that don't collect information unless the user gives permission are less invasive than "opt-out" policies that require the user to explicitly forbid this kind of tracking. The problem for the search engine is that people are less likely to bother to opt in, so it's not easy to get their cooperation. Eventually, online information systems may be able to create personalized views that are comfortable for each user so that, for example, the sales person doesn't need to know technical terminology and the researcher doesn't have to learn "market-speak."

5.3   FINDING THE RIGHT SEARCH TECHNOLOGY

Because widespread adoption of advanced search and discovery technologies is in its infancy, most buyers and users are not well acquainted with the nuances and features that distinguish various search and content analytics products. Search and content analytics technologies are best thought of as a toolbox. You don't use a screwdriver to pound in a nail, nor do you use a multimeter to check your plumbing for leaks. Similarly, you don't expect a basic search engine to discover new competitors whose names you don't know, nor do you use an eDiscovery application to tell you about marketing trends. Just like pounding in the nail with the screwdriver, you might succeed, but it will take more time, you won't do a good job, and your thumb (or your organization) will bear the unintended consequences. We discuss the search and content analytics technologies in detail in the previous chapter. In this chapter, we explore how they are used and how their effectiveness is measured.

5.3.1   FIRST QUESTIONS

Information access systems are complex because they must accommodate the variability of both language and people who have different needs and different levels of search sophistication. Most organizations decide that they need to improve information access and management and blithely set out to buy a search engine without considering what uses they will make of it. But, just as smart shoppers define what they are looking for before they head out the door, it's important to assess the information access needs of the organization before searching for search. Turning an organization with separate, disconnected information processes into one that is centered on its information will pay off. Done right, better information access can turn around an organization, increase its profits, decrease its costs, reduce wasted time, and improve its customer relations.

Rather than categorizing by type of search, information access designers need to take a step back to consider who will be using which information for what purposes. The smartest organizations start with the uses and then look for applications that will satisfy their requirements. Some of the variables to consider in assessing information access needs are:

1. What type of answer is needed in what format? All the information? Some good answers? The best and only answer? Comparisons? Tables? Trend identification over time? Reports? Charts? Graphs? Precise answers? Lists of documents? Visualizations showing relationships within an organization? Timelines or heat maps to show trends and changes? Will users need a pile of relevant documents, an analysis, a spreadsheet, a chart, a presentation, or a single data point? How soon will they need it? These are the first questions to consider, and they are rarely analyzed deeply in advance.

Search systems can return information in a variety of formats, some of which will require a lot of extra repetitive manual labor for users, and some of which will save time. For instance, even though every air carrier has its own Web site and search engine, a searcher looking for flights between San Luis Obispo, CA, and Ithaca, NY, would certainly prefer a single chart showing all carriers, all flight times, and prices. If I am trying to find out how to fix my dripping faucet, I need diagrams and a video that will show me, step by step, what to do. An attorney using eDiscovery software needs every single email that is relevant to a legal matter, categorized by topic, by name of person, and date stamped with time. Visualizing relationships among people may uncover hidden channels that indicate chicanery. If I just want to find out a bit about diabetes, complexity theory, or Impressionist painters, then one good overview article is all that I want (but it has to be good). And, if I'm looking for the viola part to a Martinu quartet, I don't want CD's, I want sheet music. These are all valid information needs, and each requires a different set of supporting technologies as well as different interaction designs.

Finding out what types of answers a system should return is tricky because people tend to think in terms of the questions they ask now, limited by the systems they currently use. It's important to ask them to dream, to describe what their answer *should* look like, in the best of all possible worlds, not how they would go about finding it.

2. Who are the intended users? Knowing the users and their tasks is imperative in designing appropriate information access systems. Are they employees who have a common culture and vocabulary? Will they be trained or are they consumers or suppliers who can't be reached with training? How many users will there be? Publishing, marketing, research and development, call centers, sales, and IT may all view the same collection of information differently. Providing multiple views, taxonomies, and terminology for the same collection of data can facilitate users' finding what they are looking for.

The question of who the intended users are is directly linked to the type of answer required, above. In developing an effective search system, it's always best—and perhaps hardest—to start by assessing the needs of the eventual users as well as the current ones because good search applications can spread through an organization like a wildfire, even if they originate in a single department.

3. What are the uses? What processes or tasks will users be engaged in and how can information finding and exploration be integrated into that workflow? Researchers may need to find other work on the same topic, or to locate an expert. Web site publishers may need to find pertinent content to rework. Marketing departments need to locate the latest approved version of corporate text or logos, while executives need to monitor competitors and market trends.

As the checklist below shows, the state of information and information processes within an organization needs to be assessed in order to plan for the size, technical requirements, and design of the future system.

5.3.2   INFORMATION NEEDS ASSESSMENT CHECKLIST

Information Needs Assessment Checklist

- Number of documents/records

- Number and type of file formats

- Number and types of sources (content management systems, file servers, databases, external sources like social media or traditional newsfeeds and data feeds, or Web sources)

- Number, rate, and type of queries projected

- Volume of information: size of existing collection and the number and rate of arrival of new records added. Larger collections need more pathways and guideposts if users are to explore them so that they can find the information they need easily. Just as I can find a book if I have only one shelf to browse, but can't locate a book in a collection of ten thousand books on fifty shelves, it's easy to find the best answer if there are ten possibilities, but it's too difficult for users to find the document they need in a list of a million documents.

- Breadth and depth of the collection. It's hard to discriminate between one document and another in specialized collections that are deep (about one topic) rather than broad. Automatic clustering and categorization work better if the discriminators among categories are very clear. In a very deep collection, the differences between one document and another may be harder to delineate. For instance, in a collection of 1 million documents about breast cancer, most of the significant terms would occur in every document. Discriminating between a document on treatment vs. one on diagnosis requires more domain knowledge, taxonomies, and better linguistic analysis, as well as tools to inspect and override inaccurate tags.

- Languages required. Which languages should be supported for search, for eCommerce, for call center interactions? Will users want to query documents that are not in their native languages? If translations are needed, how accurate must they be? How timely? What are the effects of forcing users to interact in non-native languages? In a European Union study released in 2011, only 18% of users said that they buy products online from sites that are not in their native language. The implication for eCommerce applications is clear.

- Requirements for normalizing metadata across multiple sources and formats. Most organizations have developed information silos with differing schemas and terminology. To search across these collections and merge results, some degree of term normalization is required. This can be accomplished manually or automatically, or by using a combination of the two approaches.

- Speed: must information be available instantly? Will a time lag of seconds, minutes, hours, or days make a difference in usefulness of the system?

- How quickly does the information change, and what are the requirements for indexing and archiving older materials? Stock quotes need to be up to the minute, but last week's stock prices might be valuable if one is looking at investment trends over time.

- Expertise required. Search and content analytics expertise is in short supply. For new large scale systems that use big data technologies like Hadoop, it is even harder to find skilled employees. If the skills are not easily available in-house, and the planned system is not plug and play (good search rarely is), then one must rely on either a vendor or a systems integrator. Lack of expertise for maintaining the system may also point toward using a software as a service (SaaS) version instead of trying to install it in-house. The question of expertise may also determine whether to purchase a packaged application that has already integrated all of the necessary technology and knowledge bases like taxonomies and terminology lists instead of a more generic information access platform.

- Security. Securing search is not easy. Nor is it always necessary. In general, search security—the permission to see some results but not others—is easier to control within an organization. It is usually determined by the person's role in the organization and need to know. For public facing Web sites, security is an issue for online payments, for personal information such as account number, password, or social security number. But security shades into privacy concerns when personal activities, current location, relationships, or friends are revealed. Privacy is a difficult issue, and one that has not been resolved.

- Need for continuous access to up-to-date information. Most systems require a certain amount of down time, or they may be prone to periodic outages. The degree to which this can be tolerated depends on the use. eCommerce sites can't afford down time. Consequently, they need better back up and more redundancy in their design. Small intranets, on the other hand, can probably bear the occasional outage without long-term consequences.

- Devices supported. Tablets? Mobile phones? Each may require a different format for input of a search query and a different display format for the output. For instance, if I ask for the name of a local company from my PDA, and I am driving in the vicinity, I may want directions or a phone number. If I type the same query on my desktop machine, I may be looking for current stock quote, history of the company, annual report, and list of officers.

- Software integration. Search software by definition must index collections of electronic information that were collected or created by other applications. The ease with which other collections can be connected to and searched determines how quickly a search application can be rolled out, and how current the information in the index may be.

- Vendor support. CIO's often rate vendor support and cooperation among their top considerations. In fact, in choosing a system, assuming that it could fulfill the requirements, vendor cooperativeness was the major reason many listed for selecting one product over another.

- Vendor lock-in. Does the software use proprietary formats that would require a complete reformatting and re-indexing to move to another product? Is it based on open standards so that it can input from and output to other applications?

- Price and total cost of ownership including cost of software, hardware, services, and maintenance. Note that price is the final consideration, not the first. In surveys of CIO's, IDC found that price was less important to them than the previous variables. When considering price, although this may seem obvious, it's important to know the footprint of the projected index in order to estimate the hardware requirements. Search applications vary wildly on the size of their index. It's possible to have one index exceed another in size by ten times, requiring more hardware to support it and boosting the price of the deployment. In this regard, cloud or hosted search is certainly another possibility that should be investigated.

5.4   TRADE-OFFS IN SEARCH AND CONTENT TECHNOLOGIES

The variables listed above mandate that any new system make trade-offs among them. Given the great variety of search and discovery technologies, the number of possible information-seeking tasks, and the differences in type of seeker, designing an online information system becomes a daunting task. Add to that the fact that we really don't have a definitive answer for what works best in each circumstance. Price, size of company, dependence on eCommerce, advertising, or publishing for revenue, are all parts of the equation that we have not even touched upon. It is obvious that some hard choices must be made, and that experimentation should be expected. This section lists some of the major trade-offs to consider in designing an online information system. However, even these trade-offs are not black and white: new technologies, faster processors, or cloud-based applications have started to diminish the starkness of the choice. Nevertheless, these remain questions that need to be asked in designing search systems:

- **Precision vs. recall vs. accuracy.** Precision and recall are the classic metrics that measure how well a search engine performs. Precision is the fraction of documents retrieved in a search that are relevant to a query. This is expressed as a percentage, so if I retrieve 100 documents in my search for *eDiscovery*, and only 20 are relevant, the precision of the search was 20%. Recall measures the percentage of the total matching documents in a collection that are returned. If, in my search for *eDiscovery*, there were 200 documents that would have matched the query, and I retrieved 20, the recall was 10%. "Precision" evaluates how many of the documents returned match the query, while "recall" evaluates whether the search engine has found everything in a collection that *would* match a query, whether it was returned or not. Precision and recall are usually considered to be a trade-off: if you tune for precision, your recall will go down, and vice versa. While useful, neither of these measures tells us whether the searcher will be well-served by the results. Accuracy, therefore, or perhaps utility or effectiveness, is what we are really looking for: did the search engine return the best answer in the best format to serve the needs of the user? Accuracy and effectiveness are not easy metrics. They require that we examine the information access system within the human context—purpose of search and usefulness of the answers returned within the context of the information task that a user might be engaged in.

  The context of the search—the information need, not the precision or the recall—determines the utility of the system. Did the searcher find what she needed? How hard was it to find? Some search engines give you better precision; others emphasize recall. Both are important. The intended use determines which way to tip the system, so being able to tune and improve the system is important. Precision and recall also do not take into account whether users will be able to incorporate an information system easily into the flow of a task or process in which they are engaged. These design features—the tools for interaction, exploration, and analysis—may determine whether an information access system is used, and used happily.

- **Timeliness vs. precision.** Particularly in real time monitoring of large volumes of data, it's not possible to analyze text in depth. Trend analysis for the stock market needs to be quick and accurate enough to beat the competition. It's more important to grab an emerging trend than to categorize each data point precisely if hedge funds, for instance, are to beat the market. In-depth linguistic analysis of text is computationally intensive. It requires time or large farms of processors—or both. Depth of linguistic analysis isn't necessary for applications that are looking for trends and patterns. But they should be able to handle massive amounts of data in order to confirm the patterns they find: the more data the better—as long as the need for speed isn't sacrificed.

- **UI simplicity vs. control.** User interaction design is a constant tug of war. Most users prefer simple interfaces with minimal choices—as long as they are the right choices. However, power users get frustrated if they can't control the parameters of a system. This is particularly true of taxonomy tools and tagging tools whose rule bases may occasionally yield unintuitive tags for a document. Designing for simplicity while allowing flexibility and avoiding rigidity is hard to do, but it's worth trying to please both sides. Testing alternate interfaces (on real users with real tasks to perform) early and often is the only approach that works because users, uses, and data are so variable.

- **Ease and speed of implementation vs. customization.** A basic search engine can be deployed and start indexing sources in a matter of hours. For simple applications like basic site search, this may be enough. However, if precision is important, particularly if multiple sources of information need to be integrated into a system, then some customization is required. The more accuracy you want, the higher the need for language understanding and also for domain understanding. Just as you wouldn't hire someone to answer customer support questions unless she understood company products and terms, highly accurate question answering software requires its own shelf of reference materials: lists of products, company and industry taxonomies, understanding of terms that convey sentiment related to particular products or services, and multilingual dictionaries and tools for all of these. In addition, a question must be interpreted properly. Answering the wrong question with the right answer will anger the customer, escalate the question to a human to resolve—very costly—or lose the frustrated customer to a competitor. Lists of products, specialized terms, abbreviations, acronyms, and taxonomies may have to be developed. Schemas and terminology from multiple sources and applications may need to be mapped to each other. Specialized connectors to legacy systems will have to be developed and tested. Data may be inconsistent and full of errors. Most large corporations tell us that it took them up to two years to clean up their data, even though deploying a search application took only a matter of months, including tuning it.

- **Packaged application vs. platform.** Information access platforms that provide the connectors, the file format converters, the search, categorization, and text analytics are appealing because multiple related applications that address specific information access processes can be built on top of the platform. We call these unified information access platforms. However, building these specific applications, called InfoApps, requires deep knowledge of the task and process, good interaction and UI design, and relevant taxonomies and terminology lists. Investing, for instance, in a specialized eDiscovery application package makes eDiscovery more defensible because the packaged application has already been judged effective.

- **Federation vs. central index.** Search indexes may include documents that reside in multiple sources or repositories. Or, they may simply query multiple sources simultaneously without including them in the central index. In a **federated search system**, a query is sent to multiple internal and external sources, using the connectors to each source. The search engine receives all of the answers, and integrates them into a single results set. The documents can remain in their original collections, or they can become part of a single, large collection, virtual or not. There are advantages to both approaches. Federated systems may have smaller indexes, and the source repositories can be used for other purposes. For instance, in a federated system, a transactions database will continue to function, supporting its original users directly while the results will also be supplied, when appropriate, to a central search engine. However, federated systems can be slower at query time, and calculating relevance across collections is not easy.

  On the other hand, a central index, while larger, has already normalized the data (identified similar fields, synonyms, tags, etc.), so that it returns enriched results quickly, and is often able to perform additional operations such as creating charts and graphs across multiple sources. The same amount of work on understanding the sources and their contents needs to be done, no matter where the information is stored. The choice is whether to perform operations like data gathering and normalization before query time (speeding up the process of returning relevant information, possibly highly enriched with additional metadata to improve search accuracy) or at query time so that the various sources can continue to operate as stand-alone systems. It's also possible to construct a system that queries a central index and also federates to additional sources. In this case, query processing will probably slow down performance because of the additional steps required.

- **Privacy vs. personalization.** The more an online system knows about a user, the better it performs. Personalizing a system for the interests of each individual helps the search engine to disambiguate queries, automatically suggest query improvements, and make recommendations for related information that will be of interest. On an advertising-supported site, delivering advertisements that are useful to the searcher makes the difference between "annoying" and "worth knowing." Even being able to store name, address, and credit card information for quick ordering on favorite eCommerce sites is a boon to busy people who don't want to fumble for their credit cards.

  Nevertheless, with reports of stolen data rife, people are extremely wary of having personal information stored. No one has arrived at an acceptable balance between privacy and personalization. Technologies or trusted third parties may arrive to improve the situation. Until then, an "opt-in," rather than an "opt-out" option gives the user a choice and a modicum of control.

We've now looked at the technologies, the people who might use them, and some possible search tasks. In the next section, we explore four common uses of search and discovery technologies to demonstrate how variations in use, users, and information tasks shape the application.

5.5   SEARCH AND CONTENT ANALYTICS TECHNOLOGIES: SAMPLE USE CASES

Search and discovery technologies are embedded in, or form the foundation for a myriad of applications including auction sites, Web sites, competitive intelligence or national intelligence, fraud detection, immigration, spam detection, business intelligence, recommendation engines, healthcare insurance sites, map and travel information, social media, desktop search, or product search. The following examples demonstrate the mixture of technologies, users, tasks, and goals that go into creating an online information system that is designed for a specific purpose. In each case, additional features and technologies are required beyond basic search and text analytics in order to make the application useful. These may include authoring tools, content management systems, business intelligence systems, Web analytics, administrative tools, and collaborative or social media tools.

Note that one of the key elements in each of these applications is the user interface and the interaction design. Although the underlying technologies may enable features like faceted or parametric search, the interaction designer and the UI developer must choose whether and how to use these features.

These examples vary in the following parameters:

- Number and type of users

- Type and speed of questions and answers needed

- Type of collection

- Type of information: sources, formats, and location

- Need for precision/recall/accuracy

- Need for security/privacy/personalization

- Types of access devices (desktop, mobile devices)

- Social features

- Languages/translation

- Type of value derived

- Technologies

5.5.1   WEB SEARCH

Purpose:

1. Answer any question (queries) using documents indexed from public Web sites.

2. Generate revenue by matching queries to advertisements paid for by businesses and organizations.

3. Attract a loyal following by offering cool tools and generating buzz (in order to increase ad revenue).

- Number and type of users: Anyone with an Internet connection and a device with a Web browser.

- Type and speed of questions and answers needed: Answers must be returned in sub-second time. Queries are on any topic, and answers are typically a list of documents, but the trend is toward answering major categories of questions—like driving directions, locations of restaurants, or times of flights—with an answer that is constructed from multiple sources.

- Type of collection: Large, broad, and deep. Multilingual. Growing exponentially. Change is constant.

- Type of information: Any source worldwide that is accessible by a Web crawler, including public Web sites and some proprietary databases. Information is usually in HTML format.

- Need for precision/recall/accuracy: Web search engines have settled on precision, rather than recall as their focus in delivering results because of the large number of documents that match most queries. They try to improve recall today by helping users to expand queries with drop-down lists of related queries and with type-ahead features to assist users with spelling and search phrases. However, knowing that few users browse beyond the first ten links, most Web search engine developers have decided it's more important to make those matches precise.

- Need for security/privacy/personalization: Personalization can improve search, but is often seen as an invasion of privacy.

- Types of access devices (desktop, mobile devices): Multiple devices (any).

- Social features: Web search uses link analysis, an early type of social feature that uses the popularity (number of links to it from other Web pages) of a Web page to boost or demote its ranking. Most Web search engines today are also experimenting with using social sites like Twitter, Google+, or Facebook to predict the intent or interests of the searcher.

- Languages/translation: Any language in any location. Automatic translation for non-native speakers is an important feature because many materials have not been translated.

- Type of value derived: Web search is still the major "on-ramp," or starting place, to the Web. For users, a Web search is a first step in information gathering. For individuals, businesses, and organizations whose sites are crawled, the Web attracts attention to their sites and provides a worldwide audience of potential customers. Web search engines also offer advertising space to companies to attract customers. Under some agreements, companies share advertising revenue with their customers, e.g., newspapers and other media. In the past fifteen years, this flow of query-driven advertising revenue from searchers to search engines to Web sites has created a healthy new multi-billion dollar online economy.

- Technologies: Web search is relatively straightforward in that it matches queries to documents and to advertisements, and returns them in relevance ranked order. The devil is in the details. In 2012, Google was serving 7.2 billion page views to 700 million daily visitors (Alexa estimate, July 8, 2012). The biggest challenge for Web search engines is the volume of information to index and the volume of queries they receive. Large Web search engines need massively parallel search systems with high redundancy; NLP to identify names of frequently requested people, places, events, or things; NLP for ad targeting; analytics to find top searches, best answers, geo-location; pattern detection for detecting spam; and machine learning to improve matches and spam detection.

Web Search Challenges: Web search is the Percheron of search: a workhorse that is massive in scale and yet approachable. Behind that usable exterior lies a complex infrastructure of server farms and data centers that provide enough redundancy to ensure that the service is available continuously. The search software is well tested and robust: able to handle billions of queries. What is less apparent is the cutting edge research in NLP, analytics, and big data that drive improvements and new services. Google, Yahoo!, and Bing have developed extensive NLP-based ad matching platforms for their massive advertising businesses, but also MapReduce (Google) and Hadoop (Yahoo!) to crunch and perform analytics on their search and advertising data. They use their massive collections of information to develop better machine translation, location services, and speech to text applications.

Web search engines, because they are the default on-ramp to the Web, are highly visible. That attracts business, which is almost entirely advertising based, but it also attracts attention that is both positive and negative. Here are some of the challenges that Web search engines face:

- Spam is a problem, consuming a large percentage (up to a third) of computing cycles. Because a high ranking on a Web search drives traffic to affiliate sites and advertisers, these Web sites engage in a constant game to try to optimize their pages so that they will appear at the top of the results list for a given query. In addition, "black hat" spammers try to steal valid click-through revenue through an assortment of devious strategies including paying people to click on a search result all day to boost its ranking. Web search engines are consequently in a never-ending battle to improve their anti-spam algorithms as well as to police usage.

- Competition for advertising revenue with newcomers such as social media sites threatens their revenue growth.

- Constant experiments to improve ranking and ad targeting algorithms by using additional clues about the user and the information in the collection challenge their analytics capabilities.

- Interface and interaction design experiments require large research organizations to design answer pages that deliver answers instead of lists of documents.

- Privacy is an issue because personalized search results and ads can also be seen as an invasion of privacy, creating a worldwide hue and cry in the press.

- Maintaining a benign image is difficult as search engines try to simultaneously deliver results that are perceived as unbiased and also increase their revenue from advertising.

5.5.2   ECOMMERCE SEARCH

Purpose:

1. Generate revenue by selling products to online shoppers.

2. Supply information such as product reviews, images of products, product descriptions, and customer forums to support product sales. eCommerce sites differ from online support sites in that their primary purpose is sales, not customer relationship management.

3. Increase customer loyalty.

- Number and type of users: Current or prospective customers. Anyone needing or interested in purchasing a product. A relatively small number of users compared to Web search, but depending on product and audience, larger than the average Intranet. For example, Amazon.com serves approximately 78 million visitors a day. Users are external to the company and may use any terminology in multiple languages.

- Type and speed of questions and answers needed: Questions may be about a category of product, product features and prices, or product information including reviews.

- Type of collection: Product information, product reviews, marketing information, images of products. Customer history data.

- Type of information: Structured data drawn from product databases, customer databases, and text collections of product descriptions and reviews.

- Need for precision/recall/accuracy: eCommerce search must return precise matches, but these need to be tuned not only to match a query—usually a parametric query—but to expand that query for related terms and products. Connecting the searcher with the best product quickly fuels the design of these sites so that faceted browsing, images, and rule bases for sales and marketing are all included in determining which products to display first. This is not just a matter of frequency of occurrence of terms. In fact, since the search is often of brief product descriptions in a database, frequency of occurrence may not be very useful in determining relevance.

- Need for security/privacy/personalization: Secure transactions are mandatory. Privacy and personalization are a trade-off, though customers generally appreciate being recognized and not having to type in their ordering information more than once.

- Types of access devices (desktop, mobile devices): Mobile and desktop devices are often used in different settings for different purposes. Because of their differing screen real estate, their interface designs must cater to the strengths and uses of each, with more terse information offered for the small format of a handheld device. For instance, using my mobile phone (voice interface) I may want a phone number for a company I am about to visit because I am stuck in traffic. From my desktop, I may want to know more about the company and its products. The query may be the same, though—the name of the company.

- Social features: eCommerce sites were among the first to exploit social features like customer discussion forums, as well as online chat with customer representatives. These features increase the sense that a customer is valued, and that a Web site is a welcoming and useful place to visit.

- Languages/translation: any language commonly used by customers. Machine translation is useful, but must be tuned for names of products.

- Type of value derived: Revenue from online sales. Reaches customers who may not come into a store. Good search generates more revenue. Poor search loses customers.

- Technologies: Search, categorization, and NLP are used throughout eCommerce sites, from parsing a query through creating browsing, or faceted interfaces, to recommendation engines.

eCommerce Challenges: eCommerce search is a good example of what we call an InfoApp—an application built on a platform that is search-based, but includes other technologies to make it suitable for selling products online. We know that buyers will abandon a site if they can't find what they are looking for quickly. Therefore, the site has to offer multiple alternative pathways into its product information so that users can find what they are looking for rapidly, no matter what place they start from. Furthermore, consumers expect to search using their own terminology. Consumers ask for "blue" and want to see navy, royal blue, azure, and turquoise. They ask for sweaters on British sites instead of "jumpers." They search for secateurs and are happy to find pruning shears. Pictures of products are a must. Being able to virtually try on clothing, walk around a sculpture, or rotate a piece of furniture requires specialized tools that have nothing to do with search, but everything with making a sale. And product questions must be answered with clear descriptions, but also with easy access through online chat with a customer representative.

At the same time, an eCommerce site must further the marketing and sales goals of a company by offering recommendations for related products based on what's in stock. The results must be influenced by rules for upselling and cross-selling (convincing customers that they want a more expensive product or an additional one that is related to their original search), so that relevance is a complex mixture of sales rules and terminology matches. And the products on the site must be indexed by Web search engines, even though the product information is locked up in a database that is normally inaccessible to Web crawlers. For these reasons, an eCommerce site may include any or all of the following:

- Search: Tuned for both recall and precision (find all good matches and nothing extraneous), fuzzy search to accommodate misspellings, approximate matches; parametric search to guide buyers through all of the parameters—product type, size, color—from which they can choose.

- Domain knowledge/knowledge bases of product names, terms, synonyms as well as taxonomies/ontologies for better navigation and to find related products.

- NLP for improving search by expanding queries to include synonyms.

- Categorization and NLP, particularly entity extraction, to create browsing or faceted interfaces that are like a detailed store directory.

- NLP to normalize the product information across multiple databases. Retailers with many suppliers need to map similar products together in order to display them in a single results set.

- Workflow engine: rules for understanding the buying process to determine intent, point in buying cycle (gathering information, comparing, or purchasing?).

- Merchandising applications to create and test business rules for product promotions. These must be tied to Web analytics to gauge searches for products.

- Shopping cart software for transactions.

- Secure transaction features for credit card processing and fraud detection.

- Social features may include reviews, discussion forums, online or phone chat with product representatives, all integrated with the search process.

- Web content management and publishing software, including digital asset management of images.

- Recommendations for similar as well as related products, based on taxonomies but also on rules for upsell and cross-sell.

- Inventory tracking and integration with eCommerce system to prevent sales of unavailable items and also to push overstocked items.

- Marketing software for sentiment monitoring and brand management, search engine optimization, sales, and campaign management. These tools provide marketers with data on sales trends, Web analytics, and social media sentiment and searches. They may also include campaign evaluation tools like A/B testing that lets marketers compare the effectiveness of several alternative marketing campaigns before they commit to one.

- Search engine optimization (SEO) workbench to optimize web pages, buy and track advertising. Better search engine optimization is driven by marketing rules, integrated and sometimes automated Web publishing, and analytics about customer behavior and top searches.

In eCommerce, the UI design is critical: consumers must be led to the products they want efficiently but gently. They need to be able to purchase an item immediately or to gather information about it, then return another day without having to follow the same search process again. Customers today expect that they will find what they want with a minimum of clicks and bother, and in their native languages. An eCommerce interface should include these features and more:

- Sort by field

- Faceted browse that allows drilling down by parameter to more narrow categories (e.g., shoes → men's shoes)

- Results that include images of products

- Product recommendations with reviews from other customers and from unbiased sources

- A clear process for locating products and information, and then purchasing them

- Ability to go back or undo actions

- Form filling using previously entered information

- Side by side comparisons

- Tools to try on products, or to examine them from other angles

- Choice of language

- Assurance that personal information will not be lost or used for other purposes

Shopzilla, in the screen shot below (Figure 5.1), is a typical eCommerce site that presents several possible pathways into the product information: a search box for free form queries, parametric search, images of top items in a category, promotions (free shipping), and of course a shopping cart. The inset video discusses the features of one of the shoes, and represents a trend toward using multimedia in interactive eCommerce sites.

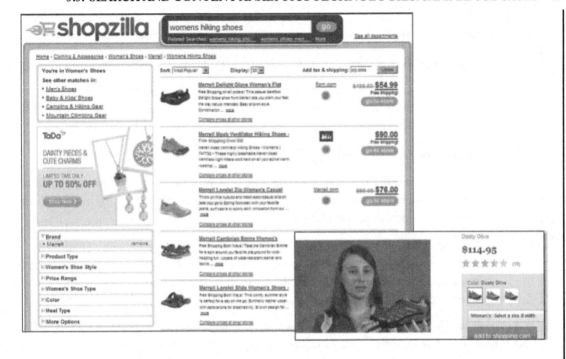

Figure 5.1: Shopzilla.

5.5.3   EDISCOVERY SEARCH

Purpose:

Provide all the pertinent electronic documents (and none that are not pertinent) to all parties to a lawsuit in a relatively speedy and legally defensible manner.

- Number and type of users: Legal counsel, opposing legal counsel, consultants.

- Type and speed of questions and answers needed: Speed is important, but sub-second speed is less important than creating a secure, interactive environment so that lawyers can get a quick sense of the number of documents that are responsive, and then begin to assess what is in the collection.

- Type of collection: Any document in any format, including email and voicemail messages.

- Type of information: Largely text documents and email messages in a variety of XML, HTML, office and email formats, although voicemail messages, pertinent images, CAD-CAM drawings, etc., must also be assessed.

- Need for precision/recall/accuracy. Both precision and recall are required for eDiscovery.

- Need for security/privacy/personalization: Security is paramount. All documents must be placed in an access-controlled collection, and must be time stamped to avoid tampering.

- Types of access devices (desktop, mobile devices): Typically, a desktop application.

- Social features: Lawyers from both parties to a legal matter need to work together for some activities, but they must discuss issues within their teams separately. Every action and decision must be tracked and recorded.

- Languages/translation: Depends on the source documents.

- Type of value derived: Highly valuable because time is of the essence. These applications can shorten the time that it takes to discover documents and plan a strategy by months. This cuts the costs for lawyers' time considerably.

- Technologies: Search, categorization, NLP, particularly for entity extraction and relationship extraction to build social graphs from email. In the case of eDiscovery, built-in knowledge bases are essential for finding company-specific terms, but above all, a well-designed user interface is imperative if the lawyer is to avoid doing repetitive work that could be avoided.

Challenges in eDiscovery: eDiscovery applications are built on a search, categorization, and often NLP backbone, but they are a good example of how a task, a process, the users, and the sources of information all affect the design of a specialized application. The application must help legal counsel discover all potentially relevant documents, from all repositories in whatever format the information exists; eliminate duplicates, but not partial duplicates; separate privileged from non-privileged documents; identify people and documents for depositions; establish the chain of custody; ensure accountability; and provide access securely across locations, languages, and time zones. The technologies and processes to support eDiscovery applications are drawn from content management, records management, knowledge management, archiving, search, workflow and process management, but with these key differences:

- The collection must include everything that is related to the matter, but nothing more. This requirement taxes search systems because it calls for high precision AND high recall. Normally these two are considered to be trade-offs, with high recall diminishing the degree of precision.

- Rules for maintaining a collection of materials involved in a legal matter are not subject to the normal rule bases of records or content management in that the materials must be frozen in time, and may not be destroyed on a normal schedule, but must wait for the litigation to be resolved.

- Access to the collection must be satisfactory to all parties to the legal matter, even though they may be opposing counsel. These applications must assist users in defining the scope, gathering pertinent data, enumerating the items, removing privileged information, and delivering the data.

eDiscovery pushes the limits of search and text analytics technologies, and presents some hard problems to application designers that are not necessarily technical, but instead have to do with the legal and business context for the process. Challenges include [Evans, 2009]:

1. The process must be legally defensible, and this is a moving target as new approaches like "predictive coding" (automated tagging using fuzzy matching, NLP, and categorization) are replacing manual coding.

2. Volume of materials. It is common for an enterprise to have amassed terabytes and even petabytes of information, but only a small percentage of their collections pertain to a given legal matter. Sifting through the volume of information quickly helps an organization decide its strategy in responding to a suit, so any eDiscovery application should be able to give a fast approximation of the amount, content, and types of possibly relevant material that may be candidates for inclusion.

3. Formats. In eDiscovery, any document is fair game, no matter its media type or format. Email in particular runs into millions of messages, often duplicating each other, that may or may not be related by an email thread. Email is often cryptic, poorly spelled, and ungrammatical. The thread provides context for messages that may continue over a period of weeks or months, but threads are sometimes not changed when the topic of conversation changes. Voicemail must be run through a speech-to-text application to transform it into text. These applications are not perfect and introduce errors of their own as they struggle with poor voice quality to understand multiple accents and voices. CAD/CAM drawings and other non-text media are difficult to integrate into an eDiscovery collection, but may be the best evidence for proving an invention.

4. Access. More and better access to the contents of each document or record opens a Pandora's box that allows endless exploration of materials from new angles. In contrast, manually coded documents can only be explored based on the original intention of the coding guidelines. Recoding manually is laborious, but online access makes it possible to add tags and reclassify documents easily and to search in a more ad hoc manner. Relationships among the entities and topics are also easier to detect in an electronic collection; unexpected relationships may be uncovered with good pattern detection software. This is a tremendous advantage for the defendants in a suit because it helps them understand quickly what their risks will be in going to court as opposed to settling. Unfortunately, opposing counsel will enjoy the same advantages.

5. Duplication. It is common to find that 50% of an eDiscovery collection is redundant. But determining if two files on two different servers or laptops are exact duplicates if they have different time stamps is not easy. Paper collections rarely have this degree of duplication. Embedded files and email attachments add to the duplication problem, with previous messages embedded in the most recent one ad infinitum.

6. Interface and interaction design. The application must be designed for ease of access and use. In eDiscovery, lawyers expect tools that allow them to oversee the automatic process and correct perceived errors. Simple issues like how to track who has examined which document, as well as tools for approving or eliminating a document, or for note taking and annotations need to be well integrated so that the rigid legal requirements of eDiscovery can be adhered to.

7. Time is a factor. As stacks of potentially pertinent materials for inclusion in any legal matter have grown, it has become necessary to automate some aspects of the process, and the volume of materials to be sorted through has spurred adoption of eDiscovery applications. In the past five years, the standard best practice for identifying materials that are responsive to a legal matter has changed from manual coding and classification to automated and machine aided approaches, today called "predictive coding." As a result of comparison tests performed in the TREC (Text Retrieval Conference) Legal Track and the Sedona Conference, standard search practice has moved from long Boolean statements to fuzzy search, categorization, browsing, and relevance ranking. These tests determined that Boolean searches retrieve about 20% of the documents that may be relevant to a case, and this may be boosted by 30% by adding a variety of fuzzy searching and NLP technologies. Defining a model for a relevant document in a less constrained system will be more difficult because it is no longer tied to a precise Boolean query that both sides have agreed to.

While eDiscovery must be a complex, well-designed application to be effective, and also legally defensible, there really is no other choice for enterprises that face multiple lengthy, expensive lawsuits. There is simply too much information. Manually sifting through it is too expensive in terms of labor and time. Moreover, humans are error prone, just as automated processes are. No approach—manual or automated—is perfect. Allowing the automated system to make the first cut, but giving people the ability to override the system appears to be the best practice today. Vendors of these products have demonstrated time and time again that automating the process saves time and money.

5.5.4   ENTERPRISE SEARCH

Purpose:

Narrowly defined, enterprise search indexes and provides access to all unstructured (and some structured) enterprise sources for all employees. Access is constrained by security and access rules that limit what employees see, based on their "need to know." To protect sensitive documents and personal information, access rights are carefully controlled. Legally defensible archiving rules purge older documents from collections and from the index on schedule, so the index must be updated to reflect the existing collection. The search system serves up documents and must supply information that is first filtered by the searcher's right-to-know: name, position, and access rights. The section below expands on this brief overview of search and content analytics technologies for the enterprise.

- Number and type of users: All employees, but in particular, executives and the marketing, sales, research, finance, legal, publishing, call center, and research and development departments.

- Type and speed of questions and answers needed: Anything from quick answers and known item searches to competitive intelligence, financial and sales status reports, customer intelligence, or expert location. Speed is less critical than it is for eCommerce search or Web search because enterprise users are a captive audience. Nevertheless, satisfaction with enterprise search is low today, and users do expect similar tools and speed to what they find on the Web.

- Type of collection: Information from all file servers, content management systems, some databases, and possibly desktop computers.

- Type of information: Information is located inside the organization in multiple locations, often in well over a hundred different sources and formats. Formats range from legacy applications and old document formats, XML, HTML, or Office formats and plain ASCII text, to columns of numbers and structured data from databases and enterprise applications.

- Need for precision/recall/accuracy: Varies with each use. Precision is necessary for known item search, but recall is needed for gathering information broadly. Both precision and recall are required for eDiscovery.

- Need for security/privacy/personalization: Security of information is paramount to protect the business from its competitors and enemies, but also to protect intellectual property. Personalization makes it easier for employees to search for information of interest to them.

- Types of access devices (desktop, mobile devices): Increasingly, access by mobile device and desktop, both inside and outside the company firewall are required.

- Social features: Information access systems are often integrated with or even embedded in major enterprise applications including collaborative tools. Employees need to find information, share and discuss it, and make decisions on their joint knowledge.

- Languages/translation: The need for support for more than one language depends on the company and its business. If the internal language is only English, then other languages need not be supported, but most companies today must deal with a multilingual world of customers, suppliers, and partners, as well as their own staff.

- Type of value derived: It's difficult to establish the value of a good enterprise search system in concrete terms. Productivity measures like number of hours saved, or projects completed more quickly are common. Several companies have begun to measure savings in terms of number of full time equivalent staff they did not need to hire and train because their employees have become more productive. Employee satisfaction is certainly another intangible but important metric.

- Technologies: Enterprise search systems typically have small-to medium-sized collections and indexes. Their complexity comes from the variety of needs they must serve, not the volume of queries or documents. They need search that can be tuned easily, categorization, taxonomies, NLP for entity extraction, good administrative tools, and search analytics tools to determine top searches and null searches (searches that yield no results). More advanced organizations are deploying full unified information access systems as the next generation of enterprise search. We describe unified information access systems in more detail in the section on trends in enterprise search, below. Briefly, unified information access systems are built on a hybrid architecture that combines features from search, and text analytics with business intelligence and database features in order to take advantage of both search and database/BI technologies.

Challenges for Enterprise Search: Unlike eCommerce systems, Enterprise search systems must support a number of tasks by a range of searchers, from personnel on the shop floor who are checking their vacation benefits, to advanced researchers who need to know prior research and find current experts on a topic. Researchers may need to find everything, but C-level executives ideally need an information system that will just alert them to the top three things they need to pay attention to that day. Because of this complex array of users and tasks, information access systems are evolving rapidly into a well-integrated set of technologies that can support multiple InfoApps, described in the next section.

5.6   SEARCH AND CONTENT ANALYTICS IN THE ENTERPRISE

The state of information access and management in the average organization today is very much in flux. Most organizations, even mid-sized ones, have at least 50-100 information repositories or collections of information. Their terabytes or even petabytes of data are growing at an alarming rate. They have multiple content management systems, each with some sort of search capability. ERP (Enterprise Resource Planning), finance, HR (human resources), customer relationship management, or call centers may each have separate access systems. Each department may depend on its own server with some information management and access tools, including a search engine as well as data warehouses and business intelligence tools. SharePoint, which has been widely adopted, has spawned additional collections of searchable information. Internal social networks and wikis have become shadow IT channels for collaboration, and they are also the repositories of the enterprise's current thinking. Large organizations have intranet search and extensive information access tools for structured information, with or without a portal. There may also be a variety of external information sources, each with its own search. The company Web site for customers and suppliers has a search engine that is usually separate from the internal search capabilities. That's the reality of enterprise information access and management today, and it's beginning to take its toll on how quickly new products or services can be developed, or how well businesses react to new opportunities or threats.

This situation isn't by design; it's evolved over a period of decades as new technologies have been enlisted to solve a particular problem, but remain to add to the complexity of the overall picture. In a way, analyzing the layers of software in any organization is like conducting an archeological dig in which new layers were added to solve the problems of the older ones, but nothing has been removed. This situation evolved slowly, and was tolerable when there were resources and funds to throw at it. However, during the past five years, and especially after the recession of 2008, organizations have been forced to reconsider the state of their IT systems, bringing the issue to a head. The layoffs of staff and spending cuts certainly helped to force the issue, but so did changes in how organizations valued their information. Research during that period, like Tom Davenport's *Competing on Analytics* or IDC's *High Cost of Not Finding Information*, changed the prevailing view of information value from dusty archive to active resource in planning and strategizing. Spending cuts may have forced IT managers to examine their expenditures and to try to figure out how to serve up information faster and better with less staff, but this sea change in how to use information (particularly unstructured information) more strategically is a motivation in itself.

Despite the recession, the increased pace of business and the growth of information in the organization have continued, adding new pressures for better information management and access.

Information work was the last bastion to resist the march of automation. But with lower budgets and less staff, CIO's are looking for ways to streamline or even automate repetitive information tasks. Call centers were one of the first areas to be attacked because the costs were prohibitive and the benefits of decreasing them by even a percent or so would be immense. Much of a call center representative's time is wasted by having to consult one information system after another, seeking answers to customers' questions. By uniting access to all of these sources through a single access point, new search systems for call centers have paid for themselves in a matter of months. Similarly, sales departments have reaped the benefits of being able to identify good prospects quickly, and to close deals faster. Marketing departments are monitoring consumer trends to create quick marketing campaigns when demand for products changes. Banks are able to identify fraudulent loan applications and to predict defaults on loans more quickly by adding text analytics to their original credit scoring software. Telecom companies can predict customer churn, picking up key phrases that are good indicators of a customer about to jump ship. Politicians can monitor how voters react to debates in real time.

Search and content analytics have assumed a prominent role in the enterprise for both finding specific items and for trolling for patterns and surprises. Although finding specific items is still important, in the enterprise, the real breakthrough for these technologies is in discovering the unknown facts, relationships, and patterns that can be mined from text. Relating information nuggets across multiple scattered sources is something that we previously relied on key longtime employees to accomplish for us. These information seers, though, can no longer keep up with everything they need to know. Search and content analytics have become a central component of enterprise computing because they provide a technical approach to handling too much information. But they are also the only reasonable approach to information problems that are not necessarily technical:

- Information is scattered across organizations, in multiple formats, in databases, on laptops, on servers and in the cloud, in ERP, CRM, HR, and a whole alphabet soup of enterprise applications. These repositories all have a purpose and a devoted following. Information is power and no one wants to give it up. Can organizations broaden access to information while continuing to allow experts to use their customary analysis and intelligence tools?

- Missed information, old information, or wrong information places the organization in jeopardy because it risks making poor decisions. Given the mountains of data that enterprises have amassed, how does an organization reduce these risks cost efficiently?

- Compliance with regulations like Sarbanes-Oxley, HIPAA, or the TREAD Act is an expensive burden that has forced organizations to reevaluate their information processes. How can they monitor messages to prevent violations, or detect and deal preemptively with problems with their products? Have they tracked data on who was authorized to see what information at what time?

- The speed of business has increased so that no one has the luxury of waiting weeks to find out how the market may have changed, what consumers are asking for, or what customers are saying. How can companies automate manual processes for monitoring customer sentiment, detecting market trends, or predicting the holiday retail season?

- New big data analysis techniques make it possible to know more, and to know it more quickly than one's competitors. Does the organization need to change its information processes and approach to avoid being out-competed?

- If information is power, how does an organization avoid the turf wars that information ownership creates?

Technology can solve some of these problems, but the organizational will to change is often the biggest obstacle to adopting newer approaches. Search and content analytics unite enterprise information by finding commonalities across repositories, then indexing everything while leaving the original information in its source application. This approach satisfies the need to have a single point of access to all enterprise information, but it also allows experts to continue to use their specialized tools. At the same time, a single point of easy access that doesn't require specialized query syntax puts business intelligence data in the hands of business users who are not business analysts. These technologies can also accommodate changes in terminology and detect trends quickly. They can provide insights into voluminous data to unveil new opportunities, as well as to prevent information disasters, like not knowing that there is a serious flaw in a product before media coverage and lawsuits do incalculable harm to a brand.

5.6.1   CONSUMER VS. BUSINESS SEARCH

Organizations that are looking for better internal search often wonder why it isn't as simple to find information internally as it is on the Web. As the examples described above demonstrate, each type of search use requires a different combination of technologies, industry and process knowledge, and interface design. The difficulty with enterprise search is that it really isn't a single problem, but rather a set of problems that must be solved with different applications that often draw upon the same set of information sources. This confuses buyers of search and discovery applications, who assume that a single solution will solve all their information access problems.

As Table 5.1 shows, businesses typically must access a greater variety of formats than a Web search engine must process, but they can expect to handle far fewer queries and documents. They also need better security and in depth exploration and analysis tools. In contrast, Web search engines face problems of scale: in users, in topics covered, in sheer volume of queries and documents. Web

Table 5.1:		
Enterprise Search	**Site Search**	**Web Search**
Topics Limited variety, all related to the organization	Company information, company products, company marketing	Broad; sometimes deep. Any topic in the world
Documents -Thousands or millions -Any format -Organized predictably	-Thousands or millions -HTML or XML format, product databases -Organized predictably, for browsing	-Billions of documents: anything on any Web site that can be crawled. Some visibility into databases -HTML or XML format -Multilingual -Not formally tagged or organized
Users -Internal, known users -Reachable for training	External customers and suppliers interested in company or products	-Anyone in the world in any language at any educational level
Queries -A few to thousands a day -Response time not as critical because the audience is captive	-Thousands a day. Possibly millions for large retail sites. -Quick response time necessary. Parametric or faceted search, images help users frame query	-Millions a day -Sub-second response time required
Security and privacy -Security of prime concern -Rights and permissions required to view search results -Secure remote access needed -Personalization an advantage	-eCommerce security for customer privacy, secure transactions -Opt-in personalization a plus for ease of ordering, finding products or information	-Personal privacy a concern -Experiments with context, user history, personalization often backfire

search engines are more concerned with privacy issues than with security of access to information, since Web search indexes contain only publicly available information, but they know perhaps too much about the interests and searching habits of their users.

Site search falls in between Web search and internal enterprise search. Site search handles lower volumes of queries and documents and a narrower set of topics or products covered than Web search does. Site search responses to queries are driven by either cost or revenue considerations (i.e., better online automatic responses save call center costs, and more relevant search and browsing generate more sales). Site search, which is the most similar enterprise search application to Web search, must still be tuned to the names of products and services that the company offers. It must make it easy for outsiders to find out about an organization, and it may be tied into eCommerce search, which has a whole different set of interactions, technologies, and processes to integrate.

In contrast, internal search systems, as we have shown in the overview of enterprise search, above, serve a disparate set of users who all have different roles in the organization and different tasks they are trying to accomplish. Businesses have different needs from consumers, making it unlikely that a simple Web search-like application out of the box can replace good search within the enterprise, although it is certainly a big leap forward from no search at all.

The question for enterprises, then, is how to address all of these information access needs—including business intelligence and financial reporting—in an economical way that allows information to flow freely through the enterprise, no matter where it resides, while also controlling access to it. Many organizations have decided to purchase ready-made, separate eDiscovery, eCommerce, intranet search, voice of the customer (sentiment analysis), marketing, and sales applications. We call these InfoApps because, inside of a single, easy-to-use workspace, they integrate the technology, the process knowledge, and the information sources that are needed for task-specific applications. InfoApps all have a strong search and discovery component, but the uses differ considerably. The advantage to buying separate applications is that they are faster to deploy, and they are fully baked to solve a specific information problem. They come with the necessary domain and task knowledge, and include specialized administrative and user tools that may need only minor tweaking to get them up and running. Easy-to-use tools for adding company terminology, product lists and/or lists of personnel are part of the package. They integrate additional technologies for collaboration, expert location, or publishing. Most important, they are well designed for a specific task, and have been tested for robustness and usability by the slings and arrows of the marketplace.

At the other end of the spectrum, some enterprises, particularly large ones that have search and text analytics experts on staff, seek an integrated single platform on which they can build the applications they want to their own specifications. Their goal is to make sure that all applications can share information, and they want to standardize multiple information access applications on a single platform in order to reduce the complexity for IT. With a single information access platform, these organizations can tag documents once and then use the results of that process for multiple purposes, from sharpening search to business and predictive analytics. Enterprises adopting this approach tend to be information-centered, with a lot to lose or gain if they don't invest in information access and analysis tools. They already have search and content analytics experts on staff, or relationships with software integrators who can provide the necessary expertise. Large financial services firms and pharmaceutical companies are good examples of this kind of enterprise.

A third, middle-of-the-road approach would be to invest in one of the new unified information access platforms that already comes with its own InfoApps, or that supplies InfoApps through partnerships with specialized applications vendors. Unified information access platforms, which we examine in more detail in the Trends section below, have developed new architectures that provide access to both structured and unstructured data. These platforms are bundled with connectors to ingest data and documents from multiple sources, and also to federate queries out to other information sources. They include easy-to-use administrative tools and tools and templates for building custom InfoApps. Because they include some popular InfoApps along with tools that allow users to customize them with taxonomies and terminology lists, it's possible to roll out applications quickly, and with less internal expertise. This approach will probably replace generic intranet search applications because it's an easy way to gain access to both structured and unstructured data, providing quick access to information and the tools to mine it.

5.7   TRENDS IN ENTERPRISE SEARCH

Designers of information access and analysis software base their products on assumptions that are prevalent in the search industry today, although they may not yet be commonly accepted in the marketplace. These assumptions create a framework for today's ideas and tomorrow's products:

- The amount of information inside and outside the enterprise will continue to grow exponentially.

- End users will be the major users of information access systems. They need help in:

    - Framing their queries clearly

    - Exploring and understanding the information that is available

    - Using the information within the context of the task they are trying to accomplish

    - Managing information overload

    - Accessing information from multiple devices and locations at any time of the day or night

    - Sharing information and tracking discussions and changes securely with colleagues and outsiders like contractors and suppliers

- Searchers want a single access point to all kinds, formats, and sources of information. They don't differentiate between information on the basis of whether it is in a spreadsheet or in a Microsoft Word document. They don't want to have to search in multiple locations using multiple passwords and protocols.

- Information seeking in the enterprise is never done in a vacuum. To be really useful, it needs to be integrated into whatever process the user is engaged in: sales, writing, marketing, strategy-setting, intelligence gathering, etc. Users want information, not lists of possibly relevant documents to leaf through.

- Information tasks are evolving from searching for information to exploring collections for the purpose of discovering trends and patterns. Tools that can facilitate discovery and exploration will help to sell information access software in the future.

- Business users are often the primary purchasers of software applications. They demand software that is easy to use and administer.

- Business users today demand access to information from a variety of mobile devices, both inside and outside of the organization. Many of these are personally owned and not controlled by the corporate IT department. Secure access is a challenge.

- Business users need to collaborate, and social tools that enable collaboration are expected to be available. If they are not, public social sites will be substituted, threatening the security of the organization.

- Open Source search and content analytics are becoming increasingly prevalent. These were originally search developers' darlings, but required extensive expertise in these technologies. Because the code is not proprietary, vendors needing to embed search in their products have used open source Lucene, Solr, Elastic Search, Gate, or OpenNLP, as well as the UIMA framework for creating an ingestion pipeline for processing and tagging text. However, new companies that support open source have begun offering tested versions that come bundled with easier administrative and development tools as well as maintenance and support. These commercially supported open source search products compete directly with proprietary search products, forcing vendors to differentiate themselves by moving to newer products: unified information access platforms and InfoApps.

A number of market influences also shape the products of the future. The following ideas and expectations are beginning to permeate the thinking of consumers and buyers of search and content analytics software and services:

- **Aggregation of content** is desirable because it's difficult to keep track of multiple sources of information or media. In this, the market has returned to the early days of traditional online services, in which services like Dialog, Lexis/Nexis, or BRS provided a common structure and set of search protocols for information from multiple sources. Newer aggregators are just coming on the scene. They make it easy to find information from multiple sources with a single search. These services are valued because they save time and enable mining of and discovery of relationships across multiple sources. No aggregator today has achieved the level of the early traditional services because there is more information available, publishers are wary of allowing their information to be merged into larger collections, and the careful curation of those early days is simply not possible in a faster moving information world. However, the need in a world of information overload is intensified. Just managing the contracts for all of the current suppliers of business information is a full time headache for large businesses that need fast access to good information.

- **Device + media in one bundle is desirable.** Access to information is most valuable to the consumer if it comes bundled with the devices that manipulate and display it. Apple's iPod and iPad are perfect examples of this synergy. These devices are inextricably linked to the Apple AppStore so that the Apps, and the device and the content are delivered in one desirable bundle. Competing device manufacturers who can't approach the breadth of the content or the applications have failed.

- **Search and BI** are two halves of the same solution. Users want information, and they don't care what format it's in or where it resides. They want a single set of tools that can be applied to all information types and that will give them a coherent view of the entire collection.

- **Filtering and personalization** in the context of a task or person improves human-computer interaction. Just as our friends recognize us and have certain expectations for what will interest or appeal to us, so must the computers and devices of tomorrow. Unfortunately, sometimes our friends are wrong, and so will our devices be.

- **Analytics** on everything. We live in a sea of data, not just from content but also from sensors, cameras, events, and users' actions, location, search history, friends, and preferences. Monitoring and mining this data enables organizations to personalize interactions with consumers, citizens, and patients, as well as to send them better-targeted bulletins, ads, and offers.

- **Big data** exploits the ad hoc and scalability features search architectures offer. Analytics pipelines using Hadoop (see section on big data below), content analytics, and inverted indices are gaining in popularity.

- **Information overload becomes information advantage** with new big data analytics that are able to mine all types of information in order to improve investments, understanding of trends, relationships between criminals, the spread of disease, and even changes in the weather.

Below are examples of how these assumptions are influencing new search and discovery applications.

5.7.1 UNIFIED INFORMATION ACCESS

Unified information access platforms index and integrate large volumes of unstructured, semistructured, and structured information into a unified environment for information gathering, processing, analysis, and decision support. Like portals and search applications, they offer rich and interactive user interface designs. Like BI applications, they integrate visual analysis tools. These platforms combine features of search, content analytics, and business intelligence to provide a single point of access to multiple heterogeneous sources of information. The architecture is new; it combines elements of the inverted index from search with BI and database features to enable analysis, visualization, and reporting. The platforms are highly scalable and are designed to accommodate quickly changing information through real-time or near-real-time updating and analytics. Because they are built on a search-like architecture, users can perform BI-like analyses on data that is retrieved with a query, building a sort of "instant data warehouse." This avoids the delays that business users endure when they want a new and different view into enterprise data.

Figure 5.2 shows a simplified view of a unified information access platform with InfoApps and interaction layers. The role of content analytics in this platform is noted on the sides.

Starting at the bottom of the software stack, a variety of data sources are ingested through connectors, tagged using text analytics, taxonomies, and other knowledge bases. They may be normalized so that similar concepts are tagged across sources. Normalized and tagged information makes it possible for users to discover relationships, common concepts, and entities among all sources. Once they have been tagged and normalized, the documents and data are indexed.

At access time, filters and knowledge bases are applied to control access, but also to present appropriate and personalized views, based on a user's role or interests. Search and BI tools, using the same architecture can perform regular searches or BI queries. The hybrid architecture allows structured data and data operators along with the classic search operations and analytics, semantic understanding, fuzzy matching, sorting, joins, and various operations such as range searching within a single architecture. This combination of the two information access worlds for text and data is very powerful, and it makes sense; it unites the strengths of both technologies so that users can apply the same tools to both information formats. Queries can be handled inside the platform, but the system can also federate a query to multiple sources and merge the results.

The two layers at the top consist of tools for interaction and interface design and the InfoApps that have been built to take advantage of the underlying unified information access platform. The interface layer provides a set of design tools with hooks into the various platform modules, and tools for designing InfoApps. The interface tools call upon the categorizers, the index, the reporting tools, the visualizers, or the analytics capabilities. They design the interactions, channeling queries and clicks to the appropriate module. InfoApps are the top layer, and they use the platform to perform specialized tasks for specific business processes like sales, marketing, finance, or eDiscovery. The InfoApps are built with the interface and platform tools, and are heavily dependent on the process engine to ease the user through the workflow of a task.

UIA platforms and their accompanying InfoApps represent a significant improvement over the separate data and content tools that are common today because they save users time, and, perhaps more importantly, they unite related information without regard to its origin or format, informing the data with supporting text, and vice versa. Because the InfoApps make it easier to interact with the system, they broaden the reach of information analysis and decision making beyond the

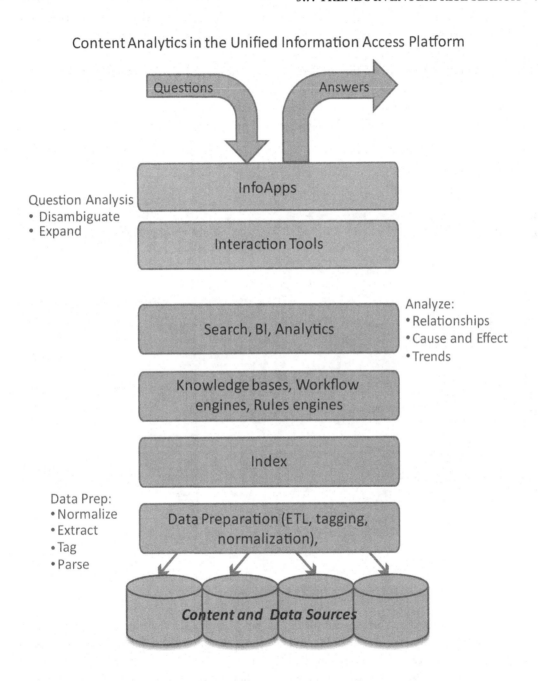

Figure 5.2: Unified information access platform.

professional searcher or business analyst. They process queries faster than traditional database and/or BI applications and add visual and graphical exploration tools. Furthermore, they are highly scalable, to terabytes and beyond.

Another strength of the unified access platform is its ability to merge information from multiple sources, bridging across multiple schemas. Unified access applications incorporate robust text analytics technologies and tools that are used at several points in the stack, as shown in the illustration below (Figure 5.3). At ingestion and processing, these technologies compare data from

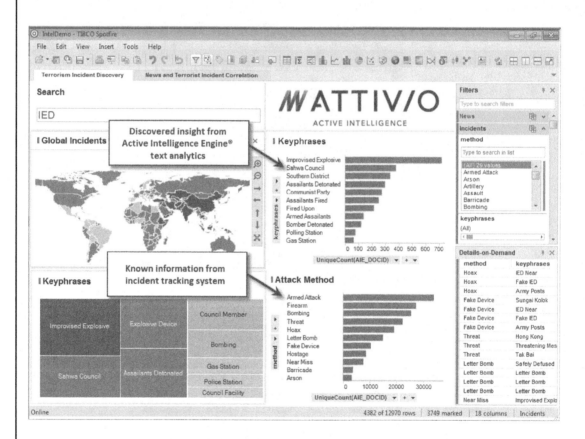

Figure 5.3: ©Attivio 2012, using TIBCO Spotfire interface.

all sources to uncover commonalities. For instance, if one database contains "customer records" and another "transactions", but both show the same customer ID numbers, text analytics tools will suggest that the two fields be mapped to the same concept. Similarly, email messages that show who a message is from or to can be mapped to other instances of a person's name, no matter where it appears, as well as to transactions in the transactions database. This process of mapping among information sources is called "normalization." It harnesses the schemas of structured data and the fuzzy matching and semantic understanding of content analytics in order to find similar items and tag them in a unified approach.

The top interaction levels are also dependent on good content analytics to interpret a query, disambiguate it and expand it, as well as to provide better interaction design for InfoApps. Once the data has been normalized and indexed, content analytics is used for sharpening search, adding browsing and faceted search to interfaces. The tagged and analyzed text that is output creates business intelligence-like analyses and reports. Figure 5.3 shows how a BI tool (Tibco Spotfire) on top of a unified information access platform (Attivio Active Intelligence Engine) can be used to visualize structured and unstructured information from multiple sources on terrorist activity. Content analytics is used to discover names of organizations in the text. Clicking on any of the bar charts lets you drill down to the original data.

5.7.2 InfoApps AND SEARCH-BASED APPLICATIONS

InfoApps, also referred to as search-based applications, provide a specialized, integrated information work environment that is specific to a process or task. These applications are designed to support a task or process. They combine multiple technologies, sources of information, and knowledge bases in a comfortable work environment that steps the user through a specific process like foraging for prospects, designing a marketing campaign, uncovering trends in spending, finding relationships among criminals, or approving a loan. Most important, InfoApps create a comfortable workspace that hides technical complexity below an easy-to-use interface.

Government intelligence and eDiscovery are two early examples of this kind of application, but any information-rich professional environment is likely to see a healthy assortment of InfoApps coming to market: in sales and marketing, search engine optimization and customer analytics, drug research, healthcare, or law enforcement, for example. These applications may be built on a unified information access platform or come as self-contained bundles of technologies and tools for information seeking and analysis, reporting and visualization, publishing, or collaboration.

InfoApps constitute the fastest growing part of the search and discovery market, and with good reason. They foreshadow a major shift in how we interact with online systems. We can view the previous two decades as the era of technology-centered applications. These applications expected the user to know a fair amount about how the technology worked in order to use it. Command line interfaces have yielded to the graphical user interface, but people still need to know how to formulate and embed an equation in a spreadsheet when all they want is to find out how their P&L is performing. The situation is akin to that of the automobile in the 1920's, and even later, when drivers had to know how to crank their autos, how to gap or change spark plugs. Aficionados gathered to discuss the finer points of magnetos, and jeered at those who were not technically inclined.

Similarly, although developers can't understand why users don't want to know how to code, most users just want to use their computers as tools that fit whatever task they are engaged in. When cars stopped being technical marvels, and just everyday conveyances that took you from A to B when you turned a key, everyone started to drive. In the next five to ten years, we will see the same thing happening to information systems: they will be embedded in everything from cars to kiosks at the mall, but the complexity will be hidden from the user, who just wants to find out what he needs to know and move on. Today, we have begun to understand human-computer interactions well enough, and the technologies are robust enough to make this dream a reality. InfoApps are an early step in this direction.

5.7.3   OPINION, TREND, AND SENTIMENT MONITORING

Monitoring what customers or constituents are saying about an organization, its activities, and its products is one of the fastest growing uses of content analytics today. Sentiment monitoring applications may be delivered as platforms, as InfoApps or as cloud-based services. They monitor social media, including the traditional media, Facebook, Twitter, and other social forums. Because the volume of messages is so large, big data technologies like Hadoop and related tools are required to mine the information. The NLP requirements are extreme because of the terse and ungrammatical nature of social media, particularly tweets. Originally, the challenges to mining tweets in particular were formidable. However, as the *The anatomy of a tweet* (Figure 5.4) below shows, there is more information in a tweet than one might expect.

These sentiment monitoring applications bundle connectors to social media with deep text analytics tools to extract names of people, products, movies, or events with the positive or negative sentiment associated with them. Today, that basic information is enriched with additional data like the name and location of the sender, or the sender's "influence" score (how influential the person is based on number of tweets and how often the tweets are re-tweeted). A typical sentiment monitoring or "listening platform" includes:

- Analytics tools to build models, develop rules

- Monitoring and alerting tools to set thresholds for alerting

- NLP for sentiment and entities

- A dashboard and reporting tools

- Administrative tools to add terminology for products and names, sites to be monitored

- Vendor support to build analyzers and to tune the application

- Tools to integrate the analyzed information into business intelligence, marketing, or decision making applications

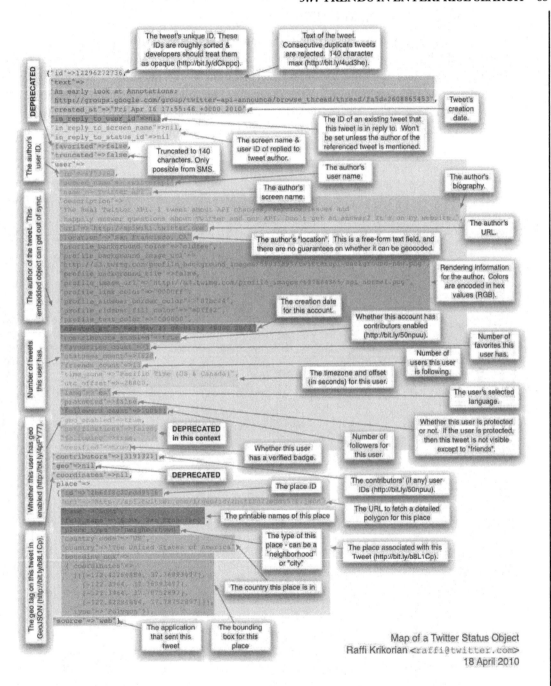

Figure 5.4: Anatomy of a tweet [Fodden, S.].

5.7.4   QUESTION ANSWERING SYSTEMS

Question answering systems are just that: they answer a question with a precise answer, not a list of documents. They may offer the answer in any format from text instructions to images, diagrams and videos or a voice response. Accurate interpretation of the question is key for two reasons: user satisfaction and cost savings for the company. The following screenshot (Figure 5.5) from eHow (`http://www.ehow.com/video_112319_fix-jammed-garbage.html`) shows how to fix a jammed garbage disposal, even though all I asked for in my query was, "how do I fix a disposal."

Figure 5.5: How to fix a jammed garbage disposal.

The search engine (Bing in this example) had to understand the question to determine the kind of answer needed (*how*, not *what is*), expand *disposal* to "*garbage disposal,*" and index videos as well as text answers.

Any time a question can be answered automatically instead of by an employee, a company saves between four dollars and more than forty dollars, depending on the level of the employee who answered the question. With questions like mine pouring into a manufacturer's Web site, the savings can add up to millions of dollars in just a few months.

5.7.5   SITE SEARCH

Site search has also received a makeover. Although we have covered eCommerce search in the previous section, Web sites are de rigueur for most companies and organizations today. Better search requires content analytics and categorization for faceted browsing. Site search is also doing a better job of trying to figure out customer intent by suggesting related searches or offering drop down menus of terms that may be of interest. Social forums and interactive help are often part of the Web site, and are linked to site search to ensure that customers are finding the information they need. Privacy is a ticklish issue because customer analytics can be viewed as an invasion of privacy, but customers also appreciate being recognized so that their results and interactions are personalized.

5.7.6   MOBILE SEARCH

The number of mobile devices today outnumbers the number of desktop and laptop computers. This trend will continue. Mobile device owners want access to information, but they are constrained by tiny screens and keyboards that are awkward to use. This set of constraints, coupled with the size of the potential market, has driven a great deal of design innovation. Information delivered to these devices must be precise and terse. It must fit the context of the user: where they are, whom they normally communicate with, what they are probably doing. For this reason, we commonly see mashups (combined applications that draw on several sources) of social and geo-location data. For instance, a device with a GPS will know where I am when I am asking for coffee, and plot the nearest coffee shops on a map of the area I am in. It may also know that I am traveling on the Massachusetts Turnpike at an uncomfortable five miles per hour and display the traffic ahead of me so that I know whether to seek an alternate route. In fact, the application may suggest an alternate route to me.

These applications require accuracy. They also require interaction design that is less cumbersome than typical typed desktop interactions. The keyboards are awkward to use, and are not suitable to situations in which the user's hands and eyes are otherwise occupied (for instance, driving a car). For that reason, applications that facilitate spoken, rather than typed interactions are rapidly gaining in popularity—witness the excitement over Apple's Siri. Speech to text technology, which fuels these applications, has been around for quite a while. By using the mobile task domain, plus an extensive and growing knowledge base, Siri can return appropriate answers, or at least delightfully wrong answers.

5.8   ENTERPRISE SEARCH SYSTEMS IN SUMMARY

Because information uses are so varied, and so poorly understood, information access systems are often ill suited to their intended uses. However, these technologies have now become central to and critical for the survival of most organizations of any size. The volume of information flooding into any organization threatens to overwhelm its employees. Although the level of sophistication in understanding these technologies has risen, it's important that buyers educate themselves about what each technology and application can and can't do. They need to understand the trade-offs to be made between precision and recall, or between trending and question answering. Trending applications require great speed over volumes of data. They need to return accurate reflections of what the majority of people are saying about a topic or a product. But the occasional outlier or anomaly should not be a problem. We are looking for what people think in the aggregate. Contrast that with the situation in a call center. In this case, we are looking at a specific individual, and trying to understand why he has called with a complaint. Aggregate numbers don't really help here: question answering systems need to answer a question perfectly, with one best answer. The trade-off is in processing an enormous volume of data quickly vs. customizing and tuning a system with much less data for answering specific questions and accurately predicting what the customer is looking for.

These trade-offs are part of designing an information access system. Different combinations of users, information tasks, interaction design, and technology are required for each type of information application.

Search technologies have progressed far beyond the search box; they may well be the new information infrastructure, replacing databases and data warehouses when massive amounts of quickly changing information need to be sifted through. Today, enterprise search vendors have moved beyond the search engine and into the more rarefied realm of interaction design, analytics, and massively scalable information access systems that will replace both traditional business intelligence and search applications.

Well-designed applications make it possible for companies to out-compete their competitors, for healthcare systems to deliver more personalized and more cost effective healthcare, and for governments to detect and assess risks. We'll examine these latter possibilities in the next section.

CHAPTER 6

Future Tense: The Next Era in Information Access and Discovery

The first section of this book examined the role of information in human interactions. In the second section, we explored the development of various technologies that help people tame the world of digital information in order to make it more manageable. But the technologies we discussed are not so easy to use, and they are a poor fit for the easy, intuitive exchange of information that is so natural to humans. In this final section, we look beyond these current technologies to consider those that are just arriving. How will these newer technologies compare to those we have now? How will they shape our information interactions, as they take the stage over the next five to ten years?

Emerging technologies will offer better options for managing and exchanging information. Although they will be embedded in practically any software that requires human interaction, they will be invisible to the user, facilitating more seamless, human-like information interactions that are well integrated into daily tasks such as information gathering, analysis, decision making, and communication.

Although we have high expectations for these newer technologies, it will take time for them to find their places in the technology pantheon. After all, technologies don't take over a market immediately, sidelining those that are well established. Instead, there is a period of experimentation. They may be used as their designers intended, or their utility may expand or contract as users play with them, finding unintended or unanticipated uses. They may be abandoned, along with other technologies that fail to live up to their promise, or they may become woven into the fabric of our work and non-work lives.

Indeed, it is difficult to predict what the landscape will look like in a decade. Although we have come a long way, advanced information access technologies are still in the technology-centric phase. Just as early automobile aficionados failed to see that the glory of the car was not its technology, but its ability to get from point A to point B with a minimum of fuss or technical knowledge, we are only beginning to shift our attention from technology to purpose. However, it is clear that the IT industry is being pushed—by increasingly vast volumes of information, globalized commerce, the governmental drive for better intelligence, and an ever-faster pace of business—to develop new types of information applications to cope with today's complex information challenges. These innovative applications will deliver more powerful digital environments that fit comfortably with the way we want to work.

Five trends have emerged that act as catalysts to the development of new types of information applications. These are:

1. Probabilistic computing

2. Learning systems

3. Big data and analytics

4. Complex highly integrated information platforms

5. Improved information interaction: contextual awareness and conversational systems

Each of these trends requires some discussion because, together, they shape how we will interact with and use information systems.

6.1   SHIFT TO PROBABILISTIC COMPUTING

Early information systems were based on certainty. They took query terms and returned exact matches; they reported number of sales and repairs. Today, the trend is toward probabilistic systems which, rather than matching queries exactly or reporting just the historic facts, have algorithms that predict the probability of a document matching a query, or a diagnosis being accurate for a patient.

Probabilistic computing predicts the likelihood that an event matches a pattern or a query and returns a score for how well the event matches. Many search engines use probability to rank search results, displaying their best approximations of a good match first. IBM's Watson creates its confidence scores based on how well the evidence it has gathered matches a question. In other words, the system collects all the possible answers to a question, and then weighs the evidence for each. Probability in this case is used to estimate the confidence of a system that an answer is correct.

This is a much harder concept to understand than the exact match, or deterministic systems, that are common today. In an exact match system, like a typical relational database, you formulate a question, and you get back anything that exactly matches that question. Every time you ask that question, you get back the same answer. That's fine for finding out the number of sales made on July 19th, and it can even compare the sales made in July 2012 to those in July 2011. What it can't find is why those sales were made. What events triggered customers to open their wallets? Are they likely to continue to either buy or not buy that product? Why?

To answer these questions, we can ask analysts to pore over the data, looking for patterns, or we can try to use technology to find correlations between sales and factors such as weather, gasoline prices, social media buzz, or marketing campaigns. Probabilistic systems look for repeating patterns. They factor in multiple elements that may not have been explicitly identified for them, based on training. Oddly enough, people behave in probabilistic, rather than deterministic ways when they make even fairly simple decisions that require weighing multiple factors, like what to make for dinner. Deciding on a menu requires knowing what's in the refrigerator, how much time there will be to shop, cook, and clean up, what everyone in the family likes and doesn't like, what was for dinner yesterday, how tired you are, what you'd like to eat, and how much you can afford to spend on ingredients. That's a lot of factors to weigh, and there is no one right answer. Many of the parameters are fuzzy (Renee won't eat anything except peanut butter, can I sneak in some vegetables?). To make a decision like this, people weigh the factors probabilistically so that they can come up with an acceptable answer that feels right. They do not analyze each choice exhaustively or overtly [Lehrer, 2009]. Similarly, given the parameters to consider, probabilistic systems can be designed to return a set of possibly serviceable or useful answers.

Probabilistic computing, applied to large collections of data, finds patterns that might not be apparent to people, who are incapable of wading through billions of documents in search of enlightenment. Because probabilistic systems return several possible answers with a confidence score, they are ideal partners in uncovering complex facts and relationships that might have eluded human experts. Experts can then take the candidate answers from the system and evaluate them. This is especially valuable in fields that have an overwhelming amount of data and in which the answer is priceless: healthcare, weather predictions, terrorism, or fraud prevention come to mind. Needless to say, the financial industry is already investing in these systems to predict investment trends as well as to reduce fraud.

This new emphasis on probabilistic computing relates to a broader, overarching trend of renewed interest in adaptive learning systems, machine learning, predictive analytics, and inferencing.

6.2   LEARNING SYSTEMS: MACHINE LEARNING, ADAPTIVE SYSTEMS, PREDICTIVE ANALYTICS, AND INFERENCING

Learning systems adapt as patterns shift or information changes. In contrast to traditional computing, learning systems are dynamic, so that they react to questions with some understanding of what the current knowledge is, rather than being tied to older data or models. Because these systems can adapt as a situation evolves, they are more agile and flexible. Probability is a necessity in learning systems, although we can't expect precision or perfection from this approach. However, learning systems are vital if we are to keep apprised of what is happening now, not three months ago. Patterns, changes, and surprises, not historical reporting, are the new focus for advanced information systems. They may use historical data as a baseline, but these systems are designed to understand a world in flux.

There are several types of learning technologies:

Machine learning technologies, and there are a number of these, find patterns in collections of information. There are two basic approaches to machine learning, and they are used for slightly different purposes:

- Supervised learning systems predict the probability that an event or a query matches a previously known pattern. Examples of events or documents are collected as training sets for the system to "learn." Patterns of salient features are detected by the system and stored. Incoming documents or descriptions of events are matched against the system and categorized based on which pattern they match best. In search and discovery, it's common to use supervised machine learning to categorize incoming documents. The drawback to using supervised learning is that selecting a training set is a time consuming process, and labeling it appropriately requires experience in how users will want to search for the topic, as opposed to other closely related topics.

- Unsupervised learning systems, in contrast, discover previously unknown patterns in collections of information. To do so, they may use machine learning technologies, but without the training data, so that the system extracts patterns that have not already been specified. Unsupervised learning may be used to bootstrap supervised learning by identifying patterns from data that can then be used to train a supervised learning system.

Adaptive systems learn from new information that is added to a system and from interactions with that information. For instance, a learning system might learn the value of an information source and adjust its weighting to reflect that value based on factors like newness or number of questions answered with a high confidence from that source.

Predictive analytics extracts patterns from a collection of data, and builds models based on a set of assumptions about how specific variables will interact. For instance, cell phone companies have built models that predict whether a customer may "churn" (move to a competing cell phone carrier) based on an incoming call to the customer service center: the type of complaint, history of use, competing offers in the marketplace, and the actual words used by the customer in expressing dissatisfaction with the service. Predictive analytics may use machine learning and other statistical techniques. The effectiveness of the model depends not only on the patterns found, but also on the accuracy of the assumptions used.

Inferencing is a technique that should be familiar to anyone who makes a decision. An inference is "a conclusion that is drawn from evidence or reasoning"(BingDictionary). It is a conclusion that is implied by facts that are known, although the conclusion may be new. People extrapolate from what they know to what might be, based on their knowledge. For instance, I can infer that ketchup and ice cream might not be a good combination, based on what I know about how each one tastes.

The importance of these technologies is that they enable information systems to learn patterns and to generalize from those patterns so that they can identify new, similar examples of them. Perhaps most significantly, learning systems adapt as new information alters or adds to what the system already knows. In other words, carefully designed, an adaptive learning system should be able to learn from its mistakes. That is in stark contrast to the static information systems of the past, but it should be a familiar behavior to humans.

6.3   BIG DATA AND ANALYTICS

Big data refers to a set of technologies and techniques for handling massive amounts of information, from specialized hardware to software, and from gathering and storage to analysis and decision-making. Although technologies like MapReduce and Hadoop attract a lot of attention in the software world, it's really the change in how we think about using massive amounts of information that will cause major shifts in the industry. We have begun to add new layers of more agile, deeper text and data analytics to business analytics. For more than half a century, we have used data in databases and data warehouses to find facts, confirm decisions or to monitor processes like sales or stock prices. Before that, of course, we used paper spreadsheets. Data have typically lived in relational databases that have a set schema and produce predictable reports. Relational databases are queried using languages like SQL that produce exact matches to a query. That's fine if you want to know sales in five states, ranked in order by number of sales, listing top items sold and the time of day when sales were highest. It's not so good if you want to identify unexpected sales trends, so that you can predict and adjust your inventory before store shelves are empty.

In other words, databases produce what you ask for, not necessarily what you should be alerted to—the surprises. They also slow down when there are too many operations to perform, or when there is too much data in multiple unpredictable formats flowing in too quickly. Preprocessing data takes time. ETL—extract, transform, and load—preprocesses data according to an established process that is not suited to variable content. Furthermore, schemas that are rigid can't accommodate demands for new views into the data because the data residing in columns and rows must be redefined in order to create a new kind of report. Finally, database technologies are not good at understanding text, which is often where the "Why?" of a problem is found. For decades, relational databases have defined the state of the art in running a business, and IT staff are comfortable with their structure, with their solid predictability and their consistency. Relational databases will continue to be workhorses in their own right, but will also be combined with other technologies to solve complex problems that require flexibility and that must handle massive volumes of data quickly.

The pace and size of business today require a speed and agility that is ill-suited to traditional database reporting. Trends and patterns need to be recognized as they emerge. Big data technologies are now emerging to handle these demands. A hedge fund that can spot a trend in rare metal investing thirty seconds before the rest of the market does can make a killing. Fraud detection at the banking window or at the loan officer's desk prevents expensive outlays of cash. Finding the causes of car crashes over hundreds of thousands of repair records prevents costly litigation and saves lives. In each of these cases, the answers do reside in the data, but we can't predict what we need to know. It's the anomalies and surprises that interest top management, and predictably formatted regular reports just confirm the valuable hunches. This new approach is neither search nor database reporting, although both technologies may contribute to the underlying information architecture. It's identification and analysis of trends, patterns, and cause and effect on a scale that the search and discovery world is only beginning to understand.

Big data technologies rely on massive amounts of data in order to detect trends and patterns statistically. Because of the size of the data sets, the chances of sampling errors are diminished. In big data applications, precision and recall may not be useful concepts. Big data thrives on a lot of data. And this wealth of data makes it possible to find statistically valid micro-segments of a population within the large data set. This gives us precision in a new sense, starting with abundant information and using it to understand events within a small segment of a population.

We can use this technique to plan the most appropriate treatment for a cancer patient by comparing our patient with others who are the same age and genome type and have already had successful treatment. In other words, we are using large amounts of data to develop more precise diagnoses. The more data we have, the higher the probability that a model is accurate. These models are then used to create more accurate micro-segments for predicting whether someone is a candidate for heart failure, likely to default on a loan or move to a different mobile phone company. They are used to spot anomalies in streams of data from hospital records and pair that information with text from news media in order to spot emerging epidemics. Manufacturers are using these techniques to identify unhappy customers who are tweeting about a repair problem so that they can contact the customers and solve the problem (and stop the negative messages). Big data techniques are also used to improve and speed up machine translation.

The problem in adopting these techniques is that people are suspicious about automated processes that supplant humans. Even though it is absolutely impossible for a team of humans to monitor all social media outlets in near real time, and to pick out from the billions of messages those relating to a specific product, many managers are reluctant to rely on a machine. Machines are consistent, but they always conform to rules, and, as we have seen, rules in the realm of language don't handle irony, jokes, or metaphors very well. In evaluating this kind of software, managers expect precision and perfection, and need to change their expectations to accept "better" rather than to demand "perfect." Users point to wrongly categorized documents or instances of a topic that are missed by the software, rather than rejoice in the abundance of newfound information that is correct. The problem is that it's easy for a computer to be foolishly consistent. Stupid computer mistakes can be real bloopers, while inconsistent human errors have a human logic behind them.

We talk about information overload as a plague. Today, attitudes toward this deluge are changing. We are beginning to realize that we can reap new benefits from massive amounts of data if we have the right tools and the right attitudes to do so. More is better if you can use great aggregations of information to mine trends and patterns that don't show up reliably in small collections of data.

6.4   IMPROVED INFORMATION INTERACTION: CONTEXTUAL AWARENESS, CONVERSATIONAL SYSTEMS, AND VISUALIZATION

For decades, we have sought to make computers more like people. The weakest spot in the man-machine relationship is at the point of interaction. Ubiquitous computing, contextually aware systems, conversational systems, pervasive computing, and intelligent agents are all different takes on the same dream—that we will be able to settle computers comfortably into the human information continuum, rather than force people to adapt constantly to the limitations of computer communication. To do so, the technologies that now absorb us, interrupt us, and confound us must become invisible. Like the best of human assistants, they must understand and support what we are doing and never intrude. Search, content analytics, and allied technologies like speech and image recognition, and machine translation are part of this dream because they enable computers to understand language, and to communicate with us in a human-like interaction. Although information gathering, organization, and analysis have been the primary purpose of these linguistically based technologies, their larger role may be to enable more optimal human-computer interaction. Three areas in particular draw upon this ability to interpret language:

Context aware systems   Context aware systems sense the state of the user's physical and digital environments in order to respond appropriately by offering information, preventing interruptions, or controlling devices [Begole, 2011]. Search and content analytics technologies provide the information by using context as a query or a filter to locate related information, make recommendations, provide driving directions, or translate text into speech, given the activity (e.g., driving a car) of the user. Context may be derived from what the user is doing, reading, searching for, or has searched for in the past. Personal profiles can add context. Context aware systems may extract location information from text and then send that information to a location-based service to find directions to a landmark. They also provide the speech recognition features to input a spoken, rather than a typed question.

Speech recognition   Human-computer interaction is awkward because it is still tied to the keyboard. People are used to talking to each other. When you interpose a keyboard, interactions become so abbreviated that it's hard to figure out what people want. But speech recognition is a difficult problem. Pronunciation varies from one person to the next, and also between regions and countries. Non-native speakers make it even more difficult. New probabilistic systems that use large collections of text are improving the accuracy of speech recognition. The next generation of interaction designs doesn't expect the computer to get it right every time. Instead, when certainty about a term sinks below a threshold, the system verifies its interpretation the way someone who is hard of hearing might, by saying, "I think you said, ___, right?"

Conversational systems   Conversational systems maintain a dialog with the user over time and can converse with humans within the context of a given task or process, very much the way we described a human dialog to get driving directions in the first section. Creating a socially adept computer is still a holy grail, but we are approaching some of these necessary characteristics as we experiment with language technologies. Conversational systems may interact through a keyboard or voice. Eventually, they may be able to respond to gestures (haptic interfaces) or even facial expressions.

A conversational system [Feldman and McClure, 2003] must be:

- Mindful and stateful: able to track a process and conversation with a specific individual over time. It must react appropriately within the context of a situation.

- Adaptive: able to understand changes in intention or direction. It must learn the user's interests to personalize responses.

- Conversationally comfortable to talk to, offering multiple modes of input and output, and an easy conversational style.

- Skilled at negotiating: able to elicit goals, offering alternatives in price, size, style, or problem solutions.

- Able to make recommendations based on the system's understanding of available alternatives and the context of the conversation.

- Socially/emotionally adept: capable of responding appropriately to a conversation at both the factual and the emotional levels. For instance, these systems are already experimenting with interpreting speech intonation patterns that indicate frustration or anger. Inferring the degree of frustration can help the system decide whether to escalate a call to a human or try to resolve the issue automatically. The system may tap the user's profile or past interaction history to identify continuing interests or names of frequent contacts. One direction that Apple's Siri has taken is to offer amusing human-like responses to soften the inability of a system to interpret a command or question correctly.

There have been a number of attempts at human-like interaction during the past fifteen years, notably in the area of customer relationship management. Automated response systems are now much-hated gatekeepers, but new advances like Apple's Siri promise to improve this situation. Figure 6.1 describes the progress from exact matching (query-response) through conceptual matching within a restricted domain like eCommerce sites, to a domain independent system that will attempt to answer any question. This last advance depends heavily on improvements in question interpretation that we will explore more fully in the IBM Watson case study.

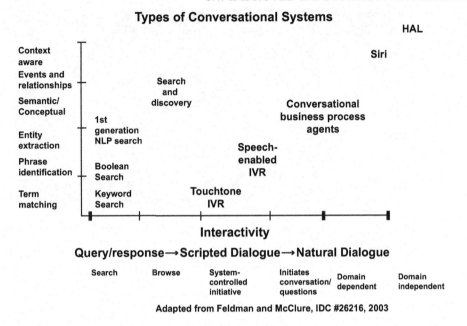

Figure 6.1: Types of conversational systems. Adapted from Feldman and McClure [2003], IDC #26216, 2003.

Visualization   Although visual representations of information are common in the world of business intelligence, they are still in an embryonic stage in the world of text. We know that size, location on the screen, color, and shape are the basic building blocks for visualizing information. What we don't know is how to present complex textual information effectively, particularly if we are trying to show large numbers and types of relationships among hundreds or thousands of entities. The default for now is to use the kinds of charts and graphs that are familiar from the business intelligence reporting world. Below are some examples of interactive information visualizations that aid exploration of large collections of information, often from multiple sources.

Google HealthMap (Figure 6.2) places incidences of a disease on a map and indicates the level of alert for each spot. The map gives context to the data in a way that a list or table never could.

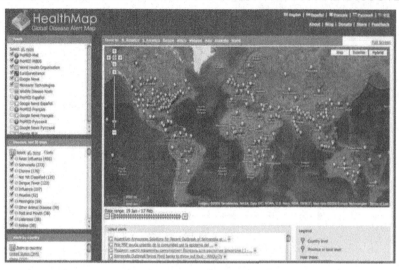

Figure 6.2: Google HealthMap.

Figure 6.3, a call center dashboard from Sinequa shows sentiment trends over time. The facets are extracted for browsing, and the bar chart shows positive/negative/neutral sentiment. All these are clickable for diving into the original data.

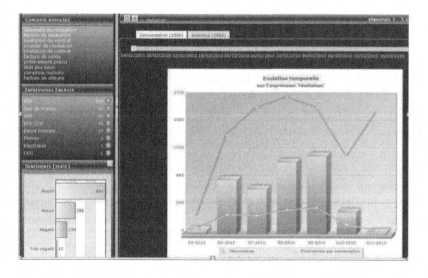

Figure 6.3: Used with permission from Sinequa, 2012.

6.5   COMPLEX, HIGHLY INTEGRATED INFORMATION PLATFORMS

Highly integrated platforms for information work incorporate modules for information ingestion, management, indexing, access, analysis, reporting, and interaction. They are the next step in the evolution from separate software applications through Services Oriented Architecture (SOA), in which the modules were united by a single protocol, but didn't communicate with each other, to a platform in which the processing outcomes in each module can affect the others.

Unified information access platforms are the first big step in this direction. Unlike portals and platforms that contain a set of modules that can be accessed separately, integrated information platforms are designed to enable the modules to interact with each other. For instance, multiple categorizers or search engines may each process the same question and then assign a confidence score that the system can use to arrive at an overall calculation of accuracy. The output from a search may fuel visualization, statistical analysis or modeling from the data retrieved without having to move from one application to another. In contrast, traditional software applications are each built around a single technology. In order to accomplish most tasks, information workers must dip in and out of a number of these applications. Each of these changes in focus interrupts the workers' task flow and ability to concentrate on a thought.

It's apparent from this overview of technologies that each one is good for some things, but not as good for others. Categorizers all differ. There have been major disagreements over which algorithm works best. Relational databases and search engines attack the problem of indexing, storing, and retrieving data differently, and each has its merits. As we saw in the previous chapter, the use, the users, the type and amount of information all determine which technology is best for each purpose.

But what if we didn't have to choose a single "best" technology? If we know some categorizers work best on broad collections, and others on deep and narrow collections, why not incorporate both into an information access system? Let them interact. Let them all attack the same problem and then return results with a confidence score for how well their results match a question. Use voting algorithms to select the best results from among several possibilities. By adding tools that are more finely nuanced, that can work together, we can build systems that address a broader range of problems.

Complex, highly integrated information platforms are the foundation for the emerging, advanced information applications (InfoApps) that are discussed in the previous section. InfoApps are designed to support a specific information-rich process, like eDiscovery, or diagnosing diseases. They use the underlying technologies in the integrated information platform, but add in the knowledge bases (taxonomies, ontologies, word lists), the pertinent collections of information that have been processed and tagged, and the user interface and tools that turn a collection of technologies into a usable application. Answer machines, which are explored in depth in the next section, go even farther along the path toward creating comfortable work environments. They make the underlying complex technologies invisible. They knit together the technologies, the processes, the knowledge, and the tools to make it easy to just get a task done.

CHAPTER 7

Answer Machines

This book has explored search and content analytics technologies, uses, and challenges as they exist today. Search is grounded in the belief that it is possible to find documents that match a query more or less accurately, and that the more the search engine understands about each indexed document in terms of what it is about, who it is by, and where and when it was published, the better our matches will be. Search is document-centric, and the process is closed off from the user. It is generally stateless, so that each successive query in an online search session is considered a separate event.

Today's search technologies are precursors to tomorrow's answer machines. In contrast to search engines, answer machines are question and questioner-centric. Answer machines try to understand the question and the motivation or intent behind the question before they match an information request to a collection of data. Focusing on understanding the question before responding is new for information systems, but it's what humans do when they exchange information with each other. This is a big step forward in online information seeking: answer machines recognize that even if two queries are the same, the two users making those queries may have different information needs.

Answer machines represent the next era of information access and analysis systems, and they embody the five large trends explored above: probabilistic computing, adaptive learning, big data, complex integrated information platforms, and contextually aware, conversational systems. Answer machines enlarge and adapt each of these trends to solve the specific challenges of information access and analysis in complex, information-rich environments. They address the following stumbling blocks described in the preceding chapters:

- Need for help in defining questions and problems.

- Need for better interaction design.

- Need for adaptive learning to adjust quickly to changing information or circumstances.

- Need for information platforms that are highly integrated so that the output from each module informs the others.

7.1 WHAT'S AN ANSWER MACHINE?

To be an answer machine, an application must meet the majority of the following criteria. Some of these are directly parallel to the general trends outlined above, but are specific to the demands of answer machines:

7.1.1   QUESTION DEFINITION

- Must be question-centric. Expands and clarifies a query before searching for answers. Engages the user in a dialog to determine the information need (the intent) that is driving the search or exploration. Agrees on the type of answer required. May use searcher's history or profile, query decomposition, classification, related terms, query expansion, or conversation with the user for this purpose.

- May formulate multiple versions of the query—hypotheses—and gather evidence to support each one to remove ambiguity. Multiple related pathways increase the chances of finding the most useful meaning by searching widely, and then narrowing the choices intelligently based on the confidence score with which each answer is supported.

- Promotes serendipity judiciously. Suggests tangentially related, possibly pertinent information to aid the user in exploring a topic. Provides browsing interfaces for exploration as well as search.

7.1.2   INTERACTION DESIGN

- Adds the searcher to the process to negotiate and clarify a question or the answers returned. Makes use of what's in the searcher's head instead of excluding the user from the process.

- Supports the entire information-seeking process from information need through query/refinement and on to analysis and use of information. Embeds information seeking, analysis, and collaboration within a larger information-dependent process, like trend analysis for business, or shopping or job seeking for personal use. This is already happening in mobile applications for finding restaurants on the go, in eDiscovery, in job seeking sites like Monster or Career Builder, or in engineering information exchanges like IHS GlobalSpec.

- Returns possible answers and the evidence for those answers. User can drill down into the evidence to discover why a result was returned.

- Personalizes the interface and the results based on the individual's interests, past history of queries, and the device used. Refines and filters both the query and the results by interests, sources, information type, history, educational level, location, current task, etc.

- Is conversational. Carries on a dialog to negotiate the query and explore the results.

- Is stateful. Tracks an information process over time to return to previous results, query formulations, analyses, visualizations, etc. Understands the predictable points in a process. For instance, someone looking for a new camera may want general information on digital versus traditional cameras, then may move on to comparing products and reading reviews. Finally, having decided to order a camera, the user will want to compare prices. In traditional search systems, every time you enter the query, "digital cameras," you will get the same results with no sense that you are picking up the process at a different point, having already digested the previous information. Stateful systems track where you are in the process to offer different types of information as appropriate.

- Loops back until the information need is satisfied, offering related areas, exploration tools, and analysis tools, rather than just a list of documents.

- Is contextually aware (of process, device in use, location, time, and other concurrent tasks) in order to deliver information appropriately.

7.1.3   ANALYTICS AND ADAPTIVE LEARNING

- Applies multiple levels of analytics at all stages of the process. Uses these to adapt algorithms.

- Learns by the success or failure of previous similar interactions. Matches new information to existing patterns to track change and to identify new categories or patterns that are emerging.

- Learns by observing usage. Measures usefulness of answers by users' reactions to them. Adapts information delivery to how the user acts on information that has been returned. Fixes errors by adjusting algorithms to avoid making the same mistake.

7.1.4   COMPLEX, HIGHLY INTEGRATED INFORMATION PLATFORMS

- Integrates multiple information access and analysis components so that they work together, not as separate modules that are federated. Like the brain, new facts and understanding must be passed around to all the different working parts. All hypotheses must be updated with new information, and recalculated to ascertain the probability that they are correct.

- Ingests, parses, analyzes, and indexes information from multiple sources in multiple formats.

- Normalizes across sources to enable system to find relationships in the data.

- Finds patterns in large volumes of information that would elude an individual. These patterns then inform suggestions made to the user.

7.2   IBM'S WATSON: AN ANSWER MACHINE CASE STUDY

IBM's Watson is a poster child for four of the major trends we have discussed: probabilistic computing, big data and analytics, learning systems, and complex highly integrated information platforms. Watson is a complex, highly integrated information platform on which IBM has built two solutions: Watson for Jeopardy and Watson for Industry. These two solutions also address the fifth major trend: contextually aware interaction design that makes the user and his feedback part of the system. More applications are in the offing, but the problems they attack all share the same characteristics—that is, large, rich, heterogeneous collections of information that span multiple sources; questions for which there is no one answer; and high stakes or high value. In these applications, the right information can save lives, save time, reduce costs, or increase revenue.

7.2.1   WATSON FOR JEOPARDY

The quiz show, Jeopardy, was Watson's proving ground, and it shaped the design of the platform. To win Jeopardy, a person or a machine must think quickly, interpret questions appropriately, and develop a strategy of how and whether to answer a question in order to win the game. The strategy changes as the game progresses, depending on the winnings of the other contestants, as well as their strengths and weaknesses. The questions are misleading and littered with word-play, innuendo, puns, rhymes, and irony. They require an encyclopedic knowledge of the world, of literature, science, history, current events, and popular culture. Questions are actually statements that need to be answered in question form. To win a round, a question must be answered as soon as a clue is read, typically after three seconds. The first contestant to "buzz in" gets to answer the question and, if correct, wins the money. Wrong answers are penalized, so speed and confidence that the answer is correct are both critical. Some sample questions taken from the Jeopardy Practice Test [Jeopardy, 2012] are (answers given in parentheses):

- Sakura cheese from Hokkaido is a soft cheese flavored with leaves from this fruit tree. (What is a cherry tree?)

- A porch adjoining a building, like where Mummy often served tea. (What is a terrace?)

- Krishna & Rama are both considered avatars of this Hindu god. (Who is Vishnu?)

- In 1903, with presidential permission, Morris Michtom began marketing these toys. (What are Teddy Bears?)

- Regarding this device, Archimedes said, "give me a place to stand on, and I will move the earth." (What is a lever?)

- In the 2007-2008 season, this Cleveland Cavalier turned 23 and averaged 30 points a game. (Who is Lebron James?)

- Atomic number 98, this radioactive element is the only one named after a U.S. state. (What is Californium?)

- Smaller than only Greenland, it's the world's second-largest island. (What is New Guinea?)

   If we look at the first question, a person (or a machine) would have to know either of the following:

1. That Sakura cheese is flavored with cherry tree leaves.

2. OR, failing that, infer the answer from:

- Where Hokkaido is located.

- What language is spoken in Hokkaido.

- What Sakura means in Japanese.

- That cherries grow on a fruit tree.

To design a system that could answer this kind of question, and do it quickly and accurately, requires integrating multiple technologies; no single technology would be adequate. Watson is a novel combination of multiple levels and types of search, content analytics and NLP, categorization, machine learning, adaptive learning, inferencing, game theory, and knowledge bases. NLP was crucial in understanding the data sources used as evidence to support the hypotheses generated by the question decomposition process. Because Jeopardy can't be won without interpreting the question properly, questions became the focus of the system design.

For DeepQA (deep question answering), as the project eventually became known, IBM recruited twenty researchers and engineers who were experts in information retrieval, NLP, computational linguistics, machine learning, knowledge representation and reasoning, and game theory [Ferrucci, 2010]. Over a period of four years, they experimented with, tested, rejected, or adapted a large swath of existing technologies. The system started with standard components including open source Lucene and UIMA (Unstructured Information Management Architecture), but these components were expanded and elaborated to the point where they were all but unrecognizable. In other words, Lucene and UIMA are to Watson what canned beef stew is to Julia Child's beef bourguignon. What Watson's creators found was that by combining multiple algorithms for each technology with a probabilistic system that could assess the odds that an answer was right, they could get the kind of performance that would give human contestants a run for their money.

7.2.2 WHAT'S UNDER THE HOOD?

Watson expands the typical search and discovery process:

1. Gathering information: Watson gathers massive amounts of structured and unstructured information from multiple sources that are germane to a specific domain.

2. Indexing information: Watson parses, tags, and indexes information deeply using a variety of NLP and statistical techniques, as well as knowledge bases, ontologies, and dictionaries. Deep preprocessing ensures that questions can be answered at multiple levels, from simple identification of entities to questions of cause and effect or pattern extraction.

3. Transforming question to query: This step is a major breakthrough in information system design. Watson deconstructs a question into its component parts. But it doesn't throw away any possible variations on the question. Whereas search engines try to disambiguate and settle on the most probable interpretation of a term, Watson pursues all interpretations as possible answers, only eliminating the least likely ones at the end. Watson's massively parallel

architecture makes it possible to look for answers to more than one question simultaneously. (As the example below shows, breaking down a question, extracting all of the entities and relationships the question contains, identifying what is missing, and then reasoning about where the answer might lie is a very complex process that humans do naturally. Teaching a computer to follow the same process is difficult.)

4. Matching the query to an index of potentially relevant responses or documents: Watson actually matches queries to answers in a series of steps, pruning the least likely, and then applying deeper levels of NLP to the remaining contenders for the right answer.

5. Ranking answers by relevance to the query: At each step, answers are given a confidence score by multiple scoring algorithms. The combined scores determine the top answers.

6. Displaying results appropriately, depending on the use.

The expanded DeepQA process looks like Figure 7.1.

The Technology Behind IBM Watson
How it Really Works

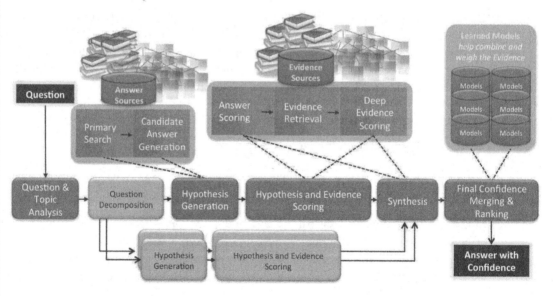

Figure 7.1: IBM Watson's Question Answering Technology.

As the diagram above shows, Watson focuses on query interpretation. In classic search this much-neglected first step almost guarantees that searchers will only find what they ask for, not what they need. Because of the deliberate ambiguity of Jeopardy questions, though, IBM researchers concentrated on getting the interpretation of the question right before they proceeded to the answering process.

Since Jeopardy demands not just the right answer, but a speedy one, Watson had to wade through mountains of information efficiently. DeepQA was therefore designed to process questions in stages so that if quick, minimal processing turned up the right answer, no further work was needed. If the question could not be answered with high confidence, the system turned to the next, deeper level of analysis. The approach of turning a question into multiple hypotheses, and evaluating each one in parallel, evolved into a design methodology that later imbued the whole system. Watson's process for answering questions is as follows:

- Deconstruct the question or the answers into their constituent parts, without any filtering; use all evaluations of what something might mean. These are the beginning hypotheses. Don't throw anything out at this stage.

- Gather evidence to support each hypothesis. Use the most appropriate and minimal technology to arrive at an initial evaluation of each hypothesis. Generate confidence scores at each stage.

- Prune to eliminate meaningless pathways quickly, and apply the next deepest level of analysis to the remaining candidates.

- Continue to iterate: evaluate evidence, compare scores, and prune further.

- Discard the least probable hypotheses at the end.

To see how this works, let's look at another Jeopardy question, "*Smaller than only Greenland, it's the world's second-largest island.*" The first step is to try to identify the type of question and the type of answer that each answer type requires (e.g., Is it a person's name? Event? Date? Comparison? A quote from a book?).

Watson's next step is to deconstruct each question into multiple hypotheses or questions, and then search for evidence to either support or disprove each one. For the Greenland question, Watson would have to:

- Parse the sentence to understand that "it" is what has to be identified.

- Extract the known facts and entities: It is an island. Greenland is an island. It is smaller than Greenland. It is larger than any island other than Greenland.

- Understand comparisons and relationships for *smaller than* and *larger than*.

- Understand that in terms of answer type, comparisons require ranking by some number. Then find the appropriate template to use for comparisons.

- Fill in the template with facts from the question: It is smaller than Greenland, but larger than any other island.

- Reason that a list of islands with various characteristics is needed.

- Understand that "second largest" relates to sizes of islands in terms of land mass, not population, or other features like height of mountains.

- Find a list of islands by size, or create such a list, and then compare them by size, choosing the one that is second in the list. Make sure that Greenland is first in this list.

Needless to say, after four years of development effort, and numerous training runs, IBM's Watson won three rounds of Jeopardy, to the delight and relief of the assembled developers. Like any contestant, Watson got things wrong, often laughably. But it was also able to "outbuzz" two human Jeopardy champions, Ken Jennings and Brad Rutter, with enough correct answers and a winning game strategy that depended on both speed and knowledge. In reviewing the matches, it seems apparent that Watson's speed in "out thinking" the other contestants may have tipped the scale. This was despite the lengths to which Jeopardy! went to prevent Watson from having any mechanical advantage. Furthermore, while human contestants may buzz in before they really have the answer, Watson has to determine the correct answer before it can buzz in. Nevertheless, the human contestants had the answers, but not the speed. Watson may also have had something that slows humans down: no need to avoid looking stupid. After all, it's hard to embarrass a computer. All three contestants were knowledgeable and fine strategists.

The Watson-Jeopardy Game did more than entertain a large audience. It brought search and discovery, learning systems, game theory, and other advanced technologies into the limelight the way a dozen speeches or white papers never would have. It also gave IBM a robust, well-tested platform on which to build practical applications. Over the next year, IBM sought ideas for how to put Watson to work, and by the end of 2011, it had launched several pilot projects. The first pilot, Watson for Healthcare, is adapted to the healthcare domain, with suitable sources of information (no movie databases, but the available medical literature, clinical trials, and genetic databases and patient records for each healthcare provider). The technology has already returned dividends, with the content analytics portion of Watson finding previously unknown patterns to predict hospital readmissions for congestive heart failure. A pilot in financial services is in the works.

In Figure 7.2, on the next page, note the use of confidence scores to guide the clinician in which treatments seem the most promising ones to pursue.

7.3   ANSWER MACHINES AND THE FUTURE

The promise of applications like IBM's Watson is that they can mimic the natural information seeking and analysis behavior of people. They can amass volumes of information and, with the right hardware, provide access to it with stunning speed. Watson hypothesizes, and then gathers evidence for each hypothesis. It reasons and infers from evidence. It learns from its successes and mistakes as well as its users' actions and feedback, and it incorporates the feedback into its next actions. Because it is not human, it doesn't reject answers based on human biases. This lack of preconceptions can sometimes lead to serendipitous discoveries.

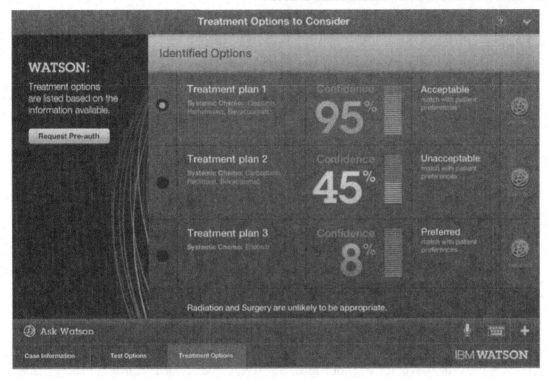

Figure 7.2: IBM Watson for Healthcare: interactive dashboard with confidence scores.

7.3.1   WHAT ANSWER MACHINES CAN'T DO

As with any revolutionary technology, humans are both excited and fearful about Watson's potential. Will it replace human judgment with harmful results? Is this the beginning of the Big Brother or Hal era? Will it take away jobs, or relegate us to being servants of all-knowing machines?

These fears are largely unfounded, as there are still many things that answer machines can't do:

- Answer machines can't halt epidemics by themselves, although they can detect—very early— patterns of infection, if they are trained to do so. Applications already exist that monitor media worldwide from local newsletters to newspapers and social media. The data are matched against hospital admissions by category in order to detect growing instances of specific infectious diseases. In fact, in the example on new kinds of interactive interfaces above, Google was able to show the spread of a virus by tracking where searches about the virus were coming from. Answer machines will be able to take this to the next level, predicting the spread of disease based on knowledge of the bursty patterns of human travel [Barabassi, 2011], and then alert public health officials when a danger threshold has been reached. Humans can then take steps to prevent the spread of disease, and they may even use answer machines to compare scenarios for different approaches to preventing an epidemic, based on historical knowledge.

- Answer machines can't answer every question in the world. Each answer machine is tied to a specific collection of information, or corpus—either for answering Jeopardy questions or for particular industries or domains, like healthcare. Like humans, each machine has to have a base of knowledge that supports understanding of a topic. A healthcare answer machine won't be able to answer questions for the auto industry. Even if it embeds predictive analytics, if its knowledge base is for predicting the weather, don't expect it to predict the outcome of the Super Bowl (although it will predict within a certain confidence level what the weather will be on Super Bowl Sunday).

- Answer machines can reason, but they can't weigh the human or societal consequences of a decision. Humans must make painful choices on whose life to save or prolong. Machines can offer the possible treatments for a condition, as well as the probability of survival for each of them. But a decision about whether to choose a painful cancer treatment must be left to the patient, who will consider his age, those who depend on him, and his desire to live.

Here's what answer machines *can* do:

- Wade through massive amounts of information more quickly than a human can.

- Navigate the complexities of human language, including such vagaries as understanding that a house can burn down while it burns up. (IBM example)

- Use vast knowledge bases to offer hypotheses about a question—a set of best guesses—based on that knowledge.

- Suggest the best possible action (among many) based on evidence that has been scored for confidence.

- Learn with each action and outcome, getting smarter as they gain experience.

- Become a digital assistant for knowledge workers who need time to understand options and make better informed decisions.

In short, answer machines can't replace or make humans redundant. But they can solve the current predicament of too much information and too little time. They are adept at analyzing collections of data and making some suggestions for action. They are not decision machines. Hard judgments and nuances, including compassion and humor, remain a purely human activity.

7.3.2 IMPLICATIONS

"A wealth of information creates a poverty of attention"
–Herbert Simon

There has always been a wealth of information for people to process. Our problem today is that in the digital world, we no longer have enough clues to tell us where to focus our attention. Answer machines can mine and organize information to help us with this attention problem. Humans are limited by their brains' processing capacity. They can't add more processors, and they don't scale up. That creates the intolerable pressures of information overload—too much information for any one person to process, integrate, and understand. However, answer machines, and big data technologies in general, thrive on more information. They demand a wealth of information in order to discern patterns and mine for nuggets. They are scalable and they don't need coffee breaks. They don't have biases or self-doubts, and they aren't embarrassed by their mistakes. They can digest and sort all the data, offering us their best estimate of what we need to pay attention to. If we couple human intelligence, real-world experience and judgment with the capacity for answer machines to crunch and evaluate information, we can break through the information overload barrier in order to make better decisions, improve medical diagnoses, and alert experts to investment opportunities, impending epidemics, or terrorist attacks.

The sum of these changes is disruption and innovation: changes in our depth of understanding and in the speed at which we are alerted to and respond to surprises. We will be able to treat our customers and patients as individuals, not forcing them to match the middle of the bell shaped curve, but taking into account their individual quirks and characteristics. In healthcare, factors like personal history, genetic makeup, home environment, or hours spent commuting will influence medical diagnoses. In business, customers will be segmented more finely to offer them products and services that more closely fit their needs. In both of these examples, the individual is the focus, but the understanding comes from the vast amount of data, segmented finely to most closely approximate a more specific set of characteristics. In other words, big data techniques allow us to handle complex decisions with more variables by virtue of the size of the data collection and the ability of the analytics tools to mine the information deeply and more specifically.

It is a foregone conclusion that businesses and organizations will gain a significant advantage if they take advantage of these new analytical approaches. We already know that organizations that rely on analytics to make decisions are outcompeting their peers [Davenport and Harris, 2007]. The successful organization expects complexity and is prepared to handle it flexibly [IBM Global, 2010].

There are non-technical, moral issues that these new technologies raise. Just because we know more facts doesn't mean that we will use them wisely. The ability to join information from multiple sources at a massive scale threatens personal privacy and smacks of Big Brother. Governments, many of which have funded the development of these technologies, are using them to wade through email, phone messages, social and traditional media, airline reservations, and money transfers to try to extract and predict patterns of terrorist attacks or fraud. On one hand, we have uncovered and prevented attacks and cut down on fraud. On the other hand, because of the prevailing and mistaken attitude that if it comes out of a computer, the information must be right 100% of the time, travelers have been detained unnecessarily, or erroneous credit records have prevented innocent citizens from obtaining loans or services. In times of disruption, social norms and the law lag behind the new possibilities unveiled by technology. We really don't know where and how to draw the line on invasion of privacy.

As we have seen in previous periods of technology disruption, there is no question that new technologies will lead to new jobs and industries, and that they will supplant well-established companies and industries. Publishing, retail sales, the post office, and the travel industry have already been disrupted. Even in those industries that have not been disrupted, many traditional knowledge worker jobs come with a new set of requirements. We need more programmers and computational linguists, but keeping up with rapid changes in technology will sideline those who don't update their skills. Companies that survive the disruption will do so because they seize new opportunities, like eCommerce, and change their business models to attract different types of customers. This is often at the cost of their established lines of business, as they end up competing with themselves, and it's a fine balancing act trying to figure out how to manage the creative destruction.

7.4 CONCLUSION

With their emphasis on the questioner and the question, answer machines stretch our understanding of how to design online information systems. How do we make information exchange easy between a machine and a human? What is the essence of human information exchange that we have not yet transferred to the online environment?

As we learn to manage and mine large data collections, we move from information overload to information advantage. This may sound like marketing hype, but the combination of better technologies with new insight into how we can use vast collections of information will make it possible for us to understand our world in ways that were simply not possible before. We are poised to leap into a new man-machine partnership, and much of it is still uncharted territory. We know that we can discover patterns and relationships that were not previously apparent in large collections of data. We are already beginning to use our newfound ability to mine data. But we have barely scratched the surface. The potential for unexpected uses, for new types of information tools, and for tools that can be used by non-specialists is vast.

The implications of answer machines for business, for organizations, and for our personal health and well-being are profound. The impact will be immense.

Bibliography

Barabassi, A. (2011) *Bursts*. New York: Penguin Group. 107

Begole, B. (2011) *Ubiquitous Computing for Business*. Saddle River, NJ: Pearson Education, Inc., publishing at FT Press. 93

Carroll, L. (1906) *Alice's Adventures in Wonderland*. New York: Cassell and Company, Ltd.

Chi, E.H., Pirolli, P., Chen, K. and Pitkow, J. (2001) Using Information Scent to Model User Information Needs and Actions on the Web. In *SIGCHI'01*, 2001 ACM.
DOI: 10.1145/365024.365325

Committee on Internal Market and Consumer Protection. Consumer behaviour in a digital environment (2011). Brussels: European Parliament. Retrieved 2012 from `http://www.europarl.europa.eu/document/activities/cont/201108/20110825ATT25258/20110825ATT25258EN.pdf`

Cross, R., Rice, R. E. and Parker, A. (2001) Information seeking in social context: structural influences and receipt of information benefits. *In IEEE Transactions on Systems, Man, and Cybernetics—Part C: Applications and Reviews* 31(4), 438. DOI: 10.1109/5326.983927

Cutting, D. (1993) Constant Interaction-time scatter/gather browsing. In *ACM Proceedings of the 16th Annual International Conference on Research and Development in Information Retrieval*, 126–134. DOI: 10.1145/160688.160706

Davenport, T. H. and Harris, J. G. (2007) *Competing on Analytics*. Cambridge, MA: Harvard University Press. 109

Downey, D. , Dumais, S. Liebling, D. and Horvitz, E. (2008) Understanding the Relationship between Searchers' Queries and Information Goals. *Conference on Information and Knowledge Management CIKM'08*. CalACM, 449–458. DOI: 10.1145/1458082.1458143

Dumais, S. (2010) Keynote: The Web changes everything: understanding and supporting people in dynamic information environments. In *Proceedings of the 14th European Conference on Research and Advanced Technology for Digital Libraries. ECDL 2010*. Berlin: Springer-Verlag.

Evans, D. (2008) Why e-discovery is a CIKM-hard problem. Retrieved 2012 from `http://videolectures.net/cikm08_evans_wediac/`

Evans, D. (2009) E-Discovery: a signature problem for search. Retrieved 2012 from Search Engine Meeting http://2009conferences.infotoday.com/documents/98/evans.pdf 67

Feldman, R. and Sanger, J. (2007) *The Text Mining Handbook*. Cambridge: Cambridge University Press.

Feldman, S. and McClure, S. (2003) Conversational Systems. *IDC publication #26216.* 94, 95

Feldman, S. (1998) The internet search-off. *Searcher Magazine*, 6(2), 28–38. 11

Feldman, S. (1999) NLP meets the Jabberwocky: Natural Language Processing. *ONLINE.*

Feldman, S. (2000) The answer machine. *Searcher Magazine* 8(1), 58 ff.

Feldman, S. (2002) This is what I asked for? The searching quagmire. In A. Mintz (Ed.), Web of Deception (chapter 9). *Information Today.*

Feldman, S. (2004) Why categorize? *IDC publication #31717.*

Feldman, S. (2009) Hidden costs of information work: a progress report. *IDC #217936.* 14

Feldman, S. (2010) Where do information workers look for information? *IDC publication #224645.* 14

Feldman, S. (2011) The answer machine: are we there yet? *Searcher Magazine* 19(1), 18–29.

Ferrucci, D. (2012) Building the team that built Watson. Retrieved 8/12/2012 from www.nytimes.com/2012/01/08/jobs/building-the-watson-team-of-scientists.html?_r=1&scp=1&sq=ferrucci&st=cse

Ferrucci, D. et al. (2010) Building Watson: an overview of the DeepQA Project. Association for the Advancement of Artificial Intelligence, Fall 2010, 59–79. 103

Fidel, R. and Pejtersen, A.M. (2004) From information behavior research to the design of information systems: the cognitive work analysis framework. *Information Research: An International Electronic Journal* 10(1).

Fodden, S. The Anatomy of a Tweet. Slaw ISSN 1925-6175. http://www.slaw.ca/2011/11/17/the-anatomy-of-a-tweet-metadata-on-twitter/, downloaded 2012. 83

Greenberger, M. (1971) *Computers, Communication, and the Public Interest*. Baltimore: The Johns Hopkins University Press.

Greffenstette, G. and Wilber, L. (2011) Search-based applications. *Synthesis Lectures on Information Concepts, Retrieval and Services*. Morgan and Claypool.
DOI: 10.2200/S00320ED1V01Y201012ICR017

Horton, F. and Lewis, S. (Eds.) (1990) Great information disasters. Bingley, UK: ASLIB

How to fix a jammed garbage disposal (2012). Retrieved 2012 from `http://www.ehow.com/`
`video_112319_fix-jammed-garbage.html`

IBM Global Business Services. (2010) *Capitalizing on complexity: Insights from the Global Chief Executive Officer Study.* Retrieved July 20, 2012 from `http://public.dhe.ibm.com/common/`
`ssi/ecm/en/gbe03297usen/GBE03297USEN.PDF 109`

IBM Watson: Ushering in a new era of computing. (2012). Retrieved 2012 from `http://`
`www-03.ibm.com/innovation/us/watson/?csr=agus_watsonopad-20120718andcm=`
`k&cr=bing&ct=USBRB301&S_TACT=USBRB301&ck=ibm_watson&cmp=USBRB&mkwid=`
`bqSzCnBd0_1457687696_432oop16376`

IBM Watson Jeopardy full episode day 1. (2011). Retrieved July 26, 2012 from `http://www.youtube.`
`com/watch?v=qpKoIfTukrAandfeature=related 102`

Ingersoll, G., Morton, T. and Farris, L. (2012) Taming Text: How to find, organize and manipulate it. Manning Early Access program, 2012. Downloaded 2012, `http://www.manning.com/`
`ingersoll/`

Lehrer, J. (2009) *How we decide.* New York: Houghton Mifflin Harcourt. 89

Lewis, D.D. and Sparck-Jones, K. (1996) Natural language processing for information retrieval. *Communications of the ACM* 39(1), 92–101.

Liddy, E. (2002) How a search engine works. In A. Mintz (Ed.), Web of Deception (chapter 10). *Information Today.*

Liddy, E.D. (1991) The discourse-level structure of empirical abstracts: an exploratory study. *Information Processing and Management* 7(1), 55–81. DOI: 10.1016/0306-4573(91)90031-G

Manning, D., Raghavan, P. and Schütze, H. (2008) *Introduction to Information Retrieval.* Cambridge: Cambridge University Press.

Marchionini, G. (2006) Exploratory Search. *Communications of the ACM*, 49(4), 41–46, New York.

Latent semantic analysis. Wikipedia. Retrieved 2012 from `http://en.wikipedia.org/wiki/`
`Latent_semantic_analysis`

Jeopardy! - Watson game 2. Retrieved July 26, 2012 from `http://www.youtube.com/watch?v=`
`kDA-701q4ooandfeature=related`

Jeopardy! IBM Watson day 3 part 2/2. (2011, February 16). Retrieved July 26, 2012 from `http://`
`www.youtube.com/watch?v=o6oS64Bpx0gandfeature=fvwrel`

Jeopardy Practice Test. Retrieved July 20, 2012 from `http://www.jeopardy.com/beacontestant/contestantsearches/practicetest`

Oard, D. (2012) *NIST TREC Legal Track*. Retrieved 2012 from `http://trec-legal.umiacs.umd.edu`

Simon, H. (2012) *Science quotes*. Retrieved 2012 from `http://www.todayinsci.com/S/Simon_Herbert/SimonHerbert-Quotations.htm`

Soygik (2012) *Map of a tweet*. Retrieved 2012 from `http://www.soygik.com/wp-content/uploads/2010/05/map-of-a-tweet.jpg`

Sparck Jones, K. and Willett, P., eds. (1997) *Readings in Information Retrieval*. San Francisco: Elsevier/Morgan Kauffmann.

Suchman, L. (2006) Human-machine reconfigurations: plans and situated actions. In *Learning in Doing: Social, Cognitive and Computational Perspectives*. Cambridge: Cambridge University Press.

Tunkelang, D. (2009) Faceted search. *Synthesis Lectures on Information Concepts, Retrieval and Services*. Morgan and Claypool. DOI: 10.2200/S00190ED1V01Y200904ICR005

Waldrop, M. (1992) *Complexity: The Emerging Science at the Edge of Order and Chaos*. New York: Simon and Schuster.

Wilson, M., Kules B., Schraefel M. and Shneiderman, B. (2010) From keyword search to exploration: designing future search interfaces for the web. Foundations and Trends®, *Web Science* (2)1. Retrieved 2012 from `http://www.nowpublishers.com/product.aspx?product=WEBanddoi=1800000003&section` DOI: 10.1561/1800000003

Author's Biography

SUSAN E. FELDMAN

 **Susan E. Feldman** Sue Feldman is Vice President for Search and Discovery Technologies at IDC (International Data Corporation), where she directs research and provides strategic advice on search engines, text analytics, categorization, unified information access, big data, visualization, and rich media search. She speaks frequently at industry events. Her research on topics such as conversational systems, big data technologies, and the high costs of not finding information has won national and international awards. She has also won awards at IDC for her mathematical models and forecasts for the digital marketplace and the search and discovery market. In 1999, Ms. Feldman wrote the chapter on search engines for the Encyclopedia of Library and Information Science and she was the first editor of the IEEE Computer Society's Digital Library News. She is a member of several advisory boards.

Before coming to IDC, Ms. Feldman was founder and president of Datasearch, an independent technology advisory firm, where she consulted on usability and on information retrieval technologies such as natural language processing, content analytics, search engines, and digital libraries. Her career began at the National Technical Information Service, where she worked with early information retrieval systems. She is a founder and former president of the Association of Independent Information Professionals, and a member of the Association for Computing Machinery.

Ms. Feldman holds degrees from Cornell University in linguistics and from the University of Michigan in information science.

Index